Window on Main Street

Window on Main Street

35 Years of Creating Happiness At Disneyland Park

Van Arsdale France

Foreword by Dick Nunis

Theme Park Press
www.ThemeParkPress.com

Editor: Bob McLain
Layout: Artisanal Text

ISBN 978-1-941500-63-7
Printed in the United States of America

Theme Park Press | **www.ThemeParkPress.com**
Address queries to bob@themeparkpress.com

Contents

PART FIVE:
The Show Goes On (1966–1970) 131

PART SIX:
Back Inside the Berm (1970–1979) 151

PART SEVEN:
Mid-Life Crisis (1979–1987) 167

PART EIGHT:
The New Era (1987–) 177

A Note from the Publisher

There are a few "holy grail" books in the world of Disney literature. These books were written by people instrumental in the success of the Disney Studio or Disneyland, and who had at least some contact with Walt Disney himself. Several such books have been out of print for decades.

Van France's *Window on Main Street* fits this category in every way. Van started work at Disneyland in 1955, dealt with Walt on numerous occasions, and was the architect of the world-famous Disneyland training programs that evolved into Disney University.

Van's book was first published in 1991. It has been out of print for a long, long time. I had to do something about that.

With help from my friend and Disney historian Didier Ghez, I was able to contact Van's daughters, Cheri France and Susan Fields. I spoke with Cheri one sultry May afternoon (sultry both here in Pennsylvania and in Cheri's small Tennessee town) and pitched the re-release of her dad's book. She was all for it. Within a few weeks, we had a deal.

Then I learned that the version of *Window on Main Street* published in 1991 was a *shortened* version of Van's book. The original manuscript was longer, more detailed. Another friend and Disney historian (can't have enough of either), Todd James Pierce, provided me with a copy of that manuscript. This was the book that Van wanted to publish. And so that's the book I *would* publish, and it's the one you hold in your hands now, a full account of Van's thirty-five years with the Disney Company.

As you read, keep in mind that Van wrote most of this book in the 1980s. He passed away in 1999. Many references in the book are dated. Most of the people who Van mentions as working for Disney are no longer working for Disney, and quite a few have sadly passed on themselves. I thought about inserting "editor's notes" like confetti throughout the book, but that would have taken you out of the story and it's important to let *Van* tell his story, without me popping up every few paragraphs to insert minutiae.

In addition to Van's daughters, I also owe a debt of gratitude to Doug Lipp, author of the best-selling book *Disney U*, and his wife, Pam, for their support of and contributions to this project.

One more thing. When I first got hold of Van's original manuscript, I noticed that it was full of ellipses...little dots separating words, seemingly at random. I thought maybe it was his distinctive writing style. But I was wrong. As Van tells it:

> My understanding of punctuation is limited...and I've never really known when a paragraph is supposed to be a paragraph. As a result...I use these little "lead dots"...when I don't know where to use a comma. And...Paul Brewer, Head of Disney's Creative Services, would say, "Here comes old 'Lead Dot'."

I've removed *most* of the "lead dots" and replaced them with commas... so if Paul Brewer ever runs into Van somewhere high above...he'll just have to come up with a new nickname for him.

Bob McLain
Theme Park Press

Foreword

I was fresh out of college when I first received a call from your author. I found him in the mass confusion of the Disneyland offices at the Walt Disney Studios.

The interview lasted about ten minutes with much of that time used up while he lit and smoked cigarettes...which I detest.

I needed a job. He offered me one at $2.00 an hour. I accepted. That two-dollar figure turned out to be only $1.80, but I was already hooked. The ten minutes began an association and friendship which survived until Van's death in 1999.

Van is a strange combination of Jiminy Cricket, Mary Poppins, and an angry Donald Duck. He believes in Walt Disney's dream of Disneyland and has convinced thousands of us that our goal is to "create happiness for others".

He goes into a Donald Duck fit if he thinks we lose sight of the dream when we have to watch costs and make a profit. To survive in this changing dream, he's mixed pixie dust with the grist of corporate reality.

He sort of conned me into doing this book, but it may be one of the best investments I ever made. At least that's what he *told* me.

For anyone interested in the history of Disneyland, Van's book is fun to read, and a one-of-a-kind for any bookshelf.

Dick Nunis
Former President,
Walt Disney Attractions
Orlando, Florida

Preface

I was born in Seattle, Washington, but moved to San Diego at the age of about 12 where my father wrote a column for the local paper, a political asset which helped me get my first decent job.

After graduating from what was then San Diego State College, I started work (at $21.00 per month) on a freighter going from San Diego to England and Canada and back. Then my grandmother helped me get a job as a dishwasher on a river boat going from Pittsburgh to New Orleans.

Coming home, a friend got me a job in a local kelp processing plant. I made 45 cents per hour, and that wasn't too bad during the Depression. Fortunately, the government came up with an unemployment program called the National Youth Administration, and I became an administrator with that organization in various parts of California.

A couple of months before World War II, I was hired as a training director by an aircraft company for what was then Consolidated Vultee, in Fort Worth, Texas.

From that time, till I went to work for Disney, my average time on any job was less then three years. I went from the aircraft company to setting up training programs for the U.S. Army in Freckleton, England, and Heidelburg, Germany, to benefit returning servicemen.

I came back to the U.S. to be hired for Kaiser's first aluminum reduction plant in Willow Run, Michigan, as a director of labor relations. Then I went back to a variety of consulting and organization jobs in southern California.

I had a dream, to set up an organization called Small Plant Management Company, which would bring my expertise to small business. A bit of a bummer. But, I made ends meet doing work for UCLA, the Navy, and—among many others—a brassiere factory.

The rest, as they say, is history...and DISNEYLAND.

About this book.

The *story* here goes back 35 years to 1954, but this book goes back 13 years, to about 1976.

Let me explain.

I had never thought of becoming 65 years old until I was 63. And here I was facing up to what at the time was Disneyland's retirement age.

Retire! Drive around in an R.V.? (I'm a lousy driver.) Play golf? (I'm terrible!) Paint the house? (I don't even own a house.) The mere idea was obnoxious to me.

Besides, I'd invested about a third of my life at Disneyland. Hell, no, I didn't want to go! Some companies let "old-timers" (a term I hate) write a book before the inevitable retirement party. It was worth a try.

I went to my boss, Dick Nunis, with the idea. He agreed, as long as it didn't interfere with my other projects.

At the time I was living on the beach in South Laguna, California. I completed my first draft, titled "Backstage Disneyland: A Personal History", and gave it to Dick. After a month or two, he read it, and I asked for his opinion, which he gave me.

"Dammit, Van, there's too much of *me* in it!" (meaning himself).

And I replied, "Hell, Dick, you've been essential to my career. How can I leave *you* out?" So I worked it over, and he took a few more months to read it, and this time he said:

"Dammit, Van, there's too much of *you* in it!" (meaning me).

And I said, "Hell, Dick, it says it is a *personal* history. How can I leave *myself* out?"

And at that time the *book* went into retirement, and *I* managed to keep working by negotiating a part-time consulting contract.

Dick then got me involved in some exciting projects: Tokyo Disneyland Training, our Disneyland Alumni Club, a program called "The Spirit of Disneyland", and other things. The book gathered dust for nine years. Then three situations caused me to think of it again:

First, at Disneyland's 30th anniversary in 1985, radio and TV people looked for "old-timers" to interview...like old war veterans. They seemed interested in the "old days".

Second, I was asked to give a eulogy for a Disney friend, which reminded me that we don't all live forever.

Third, and most important, I needed a new project to prolong my own survival.

I went to Dick with a proposal which ended up as what you'll read here.

I pointed out that most of the close friends I had made in 1955 had either died or retired, and that somebody should write a history to separate the myths from the realities.

Dick hates to think about people dying. And since he is an anti-smoking advocate, perhaps he thought I wouldn't be around too long.

In fact, since I was getting up to age 75, the thought had been crossing my mind occasionally.

At any rate, he agreed to support me and my vices until I had reworked that old, dust-covered book.

At this time, more than 200,000 people have worked at Disneyland, and every one of them has a story about the experience.

This is only one of those stories...*my story*. I'm reminded of Bill Lindley, owner of Whiskey Bill's in Newport Beach. Before beginning a joke, he'd say, "Don't stop me if you've heard this one: I want to hear it again myself."

Happy reading.

Van Arsdale France

Introduction

There are thousands of mountains in the world...there is only one Fujiyama.

There are innumerable architectural gems in the world...there is only one Taj Mahal.

There are thousands of athletic events...there is only one Olympics.

There are countless parks and entertainment sites throughout the world...there is only one Disneyland.

In various handbooks and training programs, I've emphasized that there is only *one* Disneyland and that it was the *source* for every other theme park.

But until a university professor suggested it to me, I didn't know it was a phenomenon. I had to look up the word, and settle for the fact that it is a "rare and unusual occurrence which has never happened before".

Why do I feel Disneyland is that rare and unusual occurrence. Let me count the ways...

The Timing: 1955

Disneyland might have been a flop if it had opened in any other year. It wouldn't have made it if it had opened ten years earlier, in 1945. We were just ending World War II, and *nothing* could compete with that event. It couldn't have been opened ten years later, in 1965. By that time Walt Disney's health was already weakened with cancer.

"Walt Disney: An American Original"

Bob Thomas titled his outstanding book (and my favorite source) *Walt Disney: An American Original*. Obviously, without Walt there would be no Disneyland.

The Walt-Roy Disney Brother Team

The "Disney Brothers" were a unique combination. The story is that Walt was the creative genius and Roy was the financial genius. Actually, however, Walt was credited with being one of the ten best businessmen of his time, and Roy was a great showman, which he demonstrated in the years leading up to the opening of Walt Disney World, after his brother's death.

The Baby Boom

The birth control pill had not been developed when millions of men and women came home after World War II. Between 1946 and 1964 more American babies were born than in any other period in history, and they were to be the ideal age for Disneyland.

Television

Television is taken for granted by every child today. But in early 1950 it was a miracle, and Walt Disney used it to sell Disneyland.

The Nuclear Family

Walt Disney always believed in family entertainment, and in the early days of Disneyland our society was ready to embrace a *family* park.

The "Third Wave"

In his book, *The Third Wave*, Alvin Toffler established the year 1955 as when American left its industrial society identity behind in the "Leisure Service Revolution". Most people had more money and more leisure time than at any other period in our history.

The Transportation Explosion

The interstate highway system was created in 1956, along with the creation of huge airplanes, to bring people to Disneyland.

Aside from the fact that even the Santa Ana Freeway was not completed... that there were some cities not yet created...that it took four hours to get to San Diego, and where there are no shopping malls, can you think of living without panty hose, Bermuda shorts for men, stereos, microwave ovens, frost-free refrigerators, VISA and MasterCard, disposable diapers, power lawn mowers, color TV, Versatel, the pill, the polio vaccine, electric toothbrushes, McDonald's Golden Arches, Taco Bell, or, more importantly, can you think of a world without...Disneyland.

PART ONE

From Dream to Reality

1955

ONE

I Meet Walt Disney

It was a day that changed my life. It was the day I met Walt Disney.

It was in August of 1954 and I received a call from C.V. Wood. After the usual pleasantries, he told me that he was no longer with Stanford Research, but was now working for Walt Disney as vice president of something called "Disneyland".

I asked him, "What the hell is Disneyland?"

"Why don't you drop out to my office and I'll tell you about it," was his reply. We made a date.

You may ask, "Who is C.V. Wood?" To explain, I'll have to go way back to 1941 and World War II.

C.V. Wood and I worked together for four years in Fort Worth, Texas. He was director of Industrial Engineering at the Consolidated Vultee Aircraft Corporation, and I was in charge of training. From deep in the heart of Texas, I'd gone overseas as a training specialist with the Army in England and Germany, and he'd gone west to eventually join the Stanford Research group. Our careers had occasionally crossed paths during that ten-year period, and I'd recently worked for him on a consulting job with a company which made the Whirlpool Brassiere – an interesting job.

The appointment with Wood was at four. I left my office on Wilshire Boulevard and headed out on the Hollywood Freeway to the Barham Boulevard off-ramp, and then down Riverside Drive to Buena Vista Street. At the entrance to Walt Disney Productions, a guard checked my name on a clipboard and passed me through.

Following the guard's instructions, I parked in the visitor's lot and set off on foot down Snow White Lane, past Dopey Drive, until I came to Mickey Mouse Avenue and the studio's three-story Animation Building. I walked down a hallway where the walls were decorated with Disney memorabilia and finally found Wood's secretary, who escorted me right into his office.

Always gracious, Wood got up to shake hands and then returned to a relaxed position behind his desk. Skipping the small talk, he launched directly into an enthusiastic description of how thing called Disneyland had landed him at the Disney Studio.

Woody has always been a bundle of energy wrapped in a deceptively laid-back personality. Without moving his stockinged feet from the desk top, he told me how he had come to Walt Disney from Stanford Research.

"Walt was thinking about his little Mickey Mouse Park he wanted to build across from the Studio when an architect friend suggested that he have Stanford Research do a study about the location."

Wood was so animated that he got up and walked around. "Walt and his brother Roy liked the study, and we were enthusiastic about Walt's dreams. Walt is a wonderful guy, Van, and this studio is nothing like any place you or I have ever worked. It's like a family, and Walt treats me like a son." He laughed when he said, "Roy hired me as a vice president and general manager, and when I told Walt, he said, "That doesn't leave much room for advancement."

Woody started taking off with his story. "We have FOUR MILLION DOLLARS to build this place called Disneyland down in Anaheim." Since that time I've heard other figures told about the original financing. But for me, in 1954, four million bucks seemed like all the money in the world... and that's the way I heard it.

He was just warming up about this thing called Disneyland when a dapper-looking fellow in a sport shirt entered the office and plopped down into a chair.

Without any introduction, I knew I was sitting next to Walt Disney.

With his stockinged feet still on the desk, Wood introduced me to Walt Disney. We shook hands.

I'll always remember that handshake. Somehow I'd imagined that Walt Disney would have the soft, delicate hands of an artist drawing Mickey Mouse. But my hand met the firm grip of a man who had grown up doing hard farm labor and working for his father in construction.

I had been trained that when "The Big Boss" dropped in on a lesser boss, I should politely get the hell out. But as I stood, Woody waved me back to my seat.

Disney smoked a cigarette while I was dying for one, but I was afraid to light up. He talked about the problem of explaining Disneyland to some people at the studio...and even to his own wife.

The conversation was interrupted when a small, smartly dressed man carrying a book dropped in. We were introduced. His name was Nat Wyncoff. With his book he explained the day's transactions for buying and breeding horses and ponies for the proposed park. As I listened to his report, and the ensuing conversation, I was struck by the sense of excitement Disney felt for this project. He even turned to me, an outsider, to present his thoughts. Perhaps he sensed my feeling of being uncomfortable in a strange situation.

In the back of my mind, I remembered that Woody had been involved in some crazy ideas, and he was a masterful salesman. He could easily compete with the legendary P.T. Barnum.

It was getting close to six o'clock. I waited for a good moment to leave. Woody, feet still on his desk, dismissed me, saying, "Thanks for dropping by. I'll see ya."

It was great seeing Woody again, and exciting to meet Walt Disney. I could hardly wait to tell my daughter.

Yet, like so many others, I really didn't understand what this "Disneyland" was all about. I certainly didn't know that I'd just been through a day that would change my life.

TWO

A Handshake Deal

I had forgotten about Woody and this thing called Disneyland when the phone rang one morning in my office. It was the Texan. Six months had passed since I'd talked with Woody and Walt Disney at the studio.

Woody's drawl was a clip or two faster as he explained how he'd been talking with Disney about the need for a training program for those who would operate the park now under construction in Anaheim.

"I told Walt about your work in Texas, and he agreed with me that you sounded like the guy for the job." I suppose Woody felt that if I could convert 65,000 cowboys, farmers, and homemakers into dedicated aircraft workers, then I could mold a group of diverse Californians with no business experience into producers of the "Disneyland Dream".

He got right to the point and asked if I would be interested in a consulting job. I said "yes", and we made an appointment for the next afternoon. This time Woody didn't have his feet propped up on the desk or his shoes off when I entered his office. There was a sense of urgency about the place.

I had been sandwiched in between his other appointments, but even as we talked, people kept coming and going, asking questions, dropping off architectural drawings, sometimes just walking into the room, shuffling through papers until they found what they wanted, and then walking right back out. Woody continued to stand as he talked, which was a signal that I shouldn't even *think* about sitting down. He quickly outlined the situation. His country boy drawl had speeded up to match his mood of hustle.

"We have deadlines on top of deadlines, Van. We have a firm opening date of July 17. And we're concentrating on getting the place built and finding the money to build it. It's a tough enough job just keeping the construction on schedule. But we know damn well that people have to be trained to operate the place. I know you can handle the job."

Now it was time to negotiate a fee, and I'm a lousy negotiator. In my mind, I had a figure of $200, which I didn't mention. Wood asked, "How about $200 a week?" That was the magic number. We shook hands on the deal. He told me to report to the studio the following Monday. In 1955, $200 was a good rate for a 40-hour week. I didn't know, however, that I was signing on for about 14 hours a day, seven days a week, which worked out to about $3.00 an hour.

Today, when people are interviewed for jobs, they talk about benefit programs, insurance, vacations, retirement. The only benefit I walked away with from Woody's office was the knowledge that my job might last until Disneyland opened.

At the time, however, that handshake deal seemed like a godsend. Even as the magnitude of my task become clear to me, I didn't regret my decision.

I never have.

THREE

Springtime in Burbank

The Walt Disney Studios is located in Burbank, California, not far from the "Beautiful Downtown Burbank" that Johnny Carson once made famous.

Before my first visit, I envisioned the studio as a small series of rooms equipped with skylights, which for some reason I associated with creative artists. I was totally wrong.

Actually, the studio has been called "The Campus", and with good reason. At the time of my initiation, there was the large Animation Building, surrounding by lesser buildings with names like Ink and Paint and the Shorts Building (standing for "short subjects", not underwear).

Springtime just about anywhere is a good time of year, but this one in Burbank made a special imprint on my memory. At other times, in other places, my work was with industrial factories. The structure environment of an aircraft plant, aluminum reduction plant, or auto assembly line was completely different from what I found during this chapter of my work life.

And here, wonder of wonders, were things which seemed incomprehensible to my industrialized brain:

- There were people playing ping pong, volleyball, basketball, softball, and some just lying on the grass.

- During lunch, I could hear the Firehouse Five Plus Two band, made up of animators and other creative sorts, playing music which they would later perform at Disneyland.

- I could eat lunch in a cafeteria where I might see celebrities who were working on Disney films, sharing the space, if not the table, with Walt Disney himself. And along with the usual cafeteria soft drinks there was...honestly now...BEER!

- Here there was a place I could cash a personal check, and hope it would take a few days to reach the bank.

- Here the Personnel Department was in a small, old building which was friendly, not threatening.

- Here the security officers were also friendly, and they seemed glad to see me instead of treating me as a potential crook.

To avoid commuting on the Los Angeles freeways, I rented a room at a place called the Sterling Arms, conveniently located near a bar and grill named the Olive Branch.

It was the best of times. I had a 10-minute walk down the tree-lined Riverside Drive to the studio, and a relaxing walk home.

I had always thought of "going to work" as something of a burden. Now it was exciting to get to the studio to learn something new. And, when I got back to my room, I could hardly wait to study any story about Walt Disney and his dream of Disneyland.

I was a dry sponge, soaking up Disney history at night and learning about the studio during the day. Between these periods, I could enjoy our true, but modified, spring in the days before smog became a nasty word.

At the time, I didn't realize that it was a certain quiet before the storm of Disneyland's opening.

It may have been, as I look back, one of the most productive periods in my Disneyland life.

FOUR

"A Friend in Need... Is a Friend Indeed"

I was enjoying my new life. I was also a bit scared. I was 41 years old in a totally new environment having to instantly learn a business which was foreign to me. I was surrounded by studio people who knew what they were doing. They all had their own groups of friends, and working relationships. I didn't even have anyone to eat lunch with.

But now, entering my life would be a cast of characters—individualists who would become my friends for life, and would be pioneers who would make important contributions to Disneyland's success.

C. V. Wood

On my first day at the studio in that springtime, the only person I knew was Woody, and he was too damned busy to sit around and chat about the good old times in Texas or the brassiere factory.

Woody's formal name is C.V. Wood—and I've never tried to find out what the "C.V" stands for. [Editor's note: it stands for "Cornelius Vanderbilt".] Depending on your relationship with him, and the time of day, he usually accepts "Wood", "Woody", or "C.V.".

Woody was only about 32 years old at that time, which is young for the responsibility he had been given. He was, however, one of those born leaders, and had been ever since he was a kid growing up in Amarillo, Texas. Whether it was natural or by design, he was a Texas individualist. He had graduated from Hardin Simmons University on a scholarship for—and I tell the truth—rope twirling.

By the time he reached Disney he had found a way to disarm people with his "good ol' boy" expressions. "Police station" was pronounced with an accent on the PO as POlice station, and soft drinks were called "sodee pop". Some old studio hands couldn't understand his working at an office in those stockinged feet. But his soft, brown eyes hid a mind like a computer—before there *were* computers!

He was intensely loyal to his friends, but could be as cold as steel with others. He was a pioneer whose leadership was critical for bringing Walt Disney's dream to life.

Fred Schumacher

Despite the confusion, Wood took the time to introduce me to Fred Schumacher, another pioneer who would guide me through the mysteries of my new life. Fred was about six feet two, thin, prematurely grey, ramrod straight, with a moustache which fit as though he'd been born with it. He was one of Wood's aircraft associates and an industrial engineer by profession.

No more unlikely relationship could have been created. Fred was tall; I'm not. He was precise and well-organized; I'm sloppy and moderately disorganized. He loved procedures; I hate them. He didn't drink; I do. Yet we established a working relationship which endured for years.

We had both grown up in San Diego at about the same time and could share experiences and acquaintances. He became one of my many bosses. We both enjoyed corporate politics, and I could always interrupt any major meeting if I had a rumor to share.

In the back area of Disneyland there is a Schumacher Road, one he created. Fred always had an industrial engineer's most value implement—a stopwatch—in his desk drawer. It reminded him that he could always get a job if he quit or got fired.

Fred was the first of the Disneyland pioneers to be hired, and actually had one of the rare offices. My first "desk" was the corner of a drafting table in Fred's office, with just enough room beside it for me to stand.

After a week, I was an "old-timer", and became a tour guide for new pioneers.

Dorothy Manes

Dorothy landed on the Disneyland beach head about two weeks after I did. She was greeted by Wood, who immediately took her to Fred, who immediately introduced her to me, the novice tour guide.

When Walt was planning Disneyland, one of the places he visited was Children's Fairyland in Oakland. Dorothy Manes was managing the place.

Evidently she charmed Walt, and Walt charmed her, because he hired her to organize youth activities at his park. She had grown up in San Francisco society, but after the death of her husband she moved into the world of work and Oakland politics.

I understood why Walt hired her. She had a classic look, and beneath the charming exterior was a sharp, cultured mind with a certain toughness. She was not one to be pushed around.

We became, and remained, buddies for years. She helped me with my first training program. She had a delightful sense of humor and a collection of good jokes which I still use—the cleaner ones, anyway.

Jack Sayers

Jack Sayers arrived at the studio about three days after Dorothy. His orientation differed from mine, since he went from *Walt* to Wood to Fred to me.

I introduced him to Dorothy, and we formed a threesome of sorts. And when Jack was paged a couple of times with "Jack Sayers, please call Walt", we were *very* impressed.

I found out later that Jack had known Walt for years when Jack was vice president for the Entertainment Division of the Gallup Opinion Polls. Twice Walt had asked Jack to join him in his Disneyland dream, and twice Jack backed off. He had a good job and a family to support. But the Disney charm worked, and Walt selected him to be the director of Entertainment and Guest Relations.

Jack was as tall and thin as Fred, with sandy hair and a sense of humor. They were both about my age (I learned later, about a year younger)—all in our early forties, which helped forge our alliance.

Although the studio cafeteria was the best I had ever known, eating there was no break from work. On Jack's first day, Fred suggested that we have lunch at the Olive Branch bar and grill.

With these two six-feet guys, I felt like a water boy between two basketball players. After we sat down for lunch, the waitress asked if we would have drinks.

I held back, but Jack immediately ordered a vodka and tonic, so I joined in with a scotch. Fred didn't drink, but he was not judgmental about it. As he said, "I just got sick of waking up sick and tired."

That lunch was the beginning of a relationship which would last years.

Jack Olsen

With the help of Fred, Jack, and Dorothy, I was creating our first orientation program, and I needed help for the art work and visual aids.

I mentioned my problem, and Fred introduced me to another pioneer and mentor.

Jack Olsen was a brilliant artist who had sold art supplies to Ken Peterson and the Disney Studio. Then he was hired to create the unique merchandising which Walt wanted to sell in the park. He later became the vice president of Merchandising for all of the Disney attractions. But at that time, he gave me some very wise advice.

Although Walt Disney was widely known for his insistence on quality regardless of the cost, Jack explained it very well: "Spend all the money you can on your training handbook. Then, if it *doesn't work*, Walt will know that money was not the problem. He also implied that if it didn't work, I'd probably be on the outside looking for another client.

He went on to explain Walt's philosophy about money. "Walt can be a penny pinch if he thinks money is being wasted. But perhaps at some time he had a project that failed, and lack of money was used as an excuse."

I took Jack's advice: my handbooks *were* expensive, and they worked!

Throughout the years, I continued to turn to Jack, with his brilliant mind and great talent, for sound advice.

Pulling Them All Together

I think if there's any part I've played, the vital part is coordinating these talents, and encouraging these talents, and carrying them all down a certain line.

It's like pulling together a big orchestra. They're all individually very talented. I have an organization of people who are specialists.

You can't match them anywhere in the world for what they do. But they all need to be pulled together, and that's my job.

— Walt Disney

I would meet other pioneers, make other friends, but Woody, Fred, Dorothy, Jack Sayers, and Jack Olsen were key friends who helped me through those early days.

Although some young people may never have heard of them, their contributions to those early days can still be felt at Disneyland 30 years later.

We worked together, laughed together, drank together, and helped each other in our different responsibilities.

It is true that "a friend in need is a friend indeed".

FIVE

Learning "The Ropes at Disney"

I had created training programs for Rosie the Riveter and other people in heavy industry, but here I was developing a program for people operating a crazy dream. I explained my problem to Fred, and he arranged for me to meet Ken Siedling, the head of the studio Personnel Department.

Ken was a medium-sized man with a friendly, puckish smile who ran the Personnel Department from a small frame building near the Security entrance. He exuded none of the self-importance you sometimes find in people who have control over the hiring and firing of others. His desk was the kind I liked—cluttered. When I said I was doing a handbook for Disney, he dug around and found a small book for studio people: *The Ropes at Disney*.

It showed Goofy and Mickey pulling the ropes backstage in a theater, and it covered the rules in a light way. Since Walt had obviously approved it, I felt that I could get by using a light touch in the Disneyland handbook. In addition to lending me *The Ropes at Disney*, Ken also gave me some friendly tips about the unique Disney ways of working.

Some committee-managed companies talk of their "corporate culture". Here, the traditions were what Walt *said* they were—and what I heard, I liked.

First Names

Walt insisted that people call each other, and him, by their first names. His response to being called "Mr. Disney" was, "My *father* is Mr. Disney." This was tough for me. I'd been raised in formal corporations where you didn't use people's first names unless you knew them personally.

"No Geniuses at the Studio"

Walt didn't like pretentious, status-seeking, title-happy people or stuffed shirts. He either put them down or got rid of them.

Offices

Walt hated to spend money on things his audiences couldn't see. The office desks and equipment looked as though they had been purchased at a war surplus sale—from World War I.

Organization Charts

Fortunately, someone told me that Walt hated organization charts. Unfortunately, I'd become very good at these things, so it was a talent down the tubes. I'll never know why Walt hated these charts with lines and boxes showing who was supposed to do what. My *guess* is that Walt felt such industrialized structures inhibited teamwork and creative efforts.

Drinking and Smoking

Walt smoked, and in those days many of the rest of us did, too. And drinking was OK, off the job, if it didn't interfere with your work. My kind of place.

I learned to like this seemingly unstructured way of working. You could never say, "It's not my job," despite that in reality there was a structure which could be felt, if not seen.

···

Milt Albright: Savior in the Shorts Building

Back in 1955 there were no credit cards as we now know them. There were no "instance cash" machines. Bankers still kept "banker's hours". If you were broke, you were out of luck.

And one day I was broke...out of eating and drinking money. I tried to borrow a few bucks from Fred, but he suggested that I go see Milt Albright, who handled all accounting in the Shorts Building.

Never in my past experience had I worked in a place where you could cash a check. I introduced myself to this friendly man and told him my situation. "No problem," he said. And he cashed my check...post-dated, I must admit. And from then until now we've been friends and colleagues.

We are, in fact, members of an exclusive and secret fraternal organization I call the DAOOF: Disneyland Association Of Old Farts. Milt's contributions have been numerous, including being the founder of the Magic Kingdom Club.

···

SIX

The Trainer Gets Trained

Although I was a neophyte among the old studio hands, I was gradually learning the necessary ropes for survival.

I knew the best times to go to the studio cafeteria. And when I left work in the evening, the bartender at the Olive Branch knew me, as did the waitress—essential contacts.

At the studio, I had found a restroom which was never used except when the Mouseketeers were rehearsing, and that room served as my office when somebody else was using the corner of the drafting board in Fred's office.

I am an expert scrounger, and I picked up every bit of Disney lore I could find, which I researched in the evenings.

But when people asked me, "What is this Disneyland?" I was not too sharp with the answer. The head trainer for future Disneyland workers—me—needed some training.

My first, and only, classroom orientation was to be presented by Nat Wyncoff, with two executives, one from Eastman Kodak and one from the Carnation Company. I had met Nat that first day when I'd met Walt. He was a "pitchman" and a damned good one. He could have been picked by Central Casting as a Hollywood promoter.

Nat's only prop was an original oil painting produced by Peter Ellenshaw, the creative artist who had won an Academy Award for *20,000 Leagues Under the Sea*. It was also the painting which Walt used for progress reports on the *Disneyland* TV show.

But it was a very impressive presentation which has stuck in my memory bank until today.

Since that morning in January of 1955, I had read about and heard about and written about various versions of the creation of Disneyland. Here is what I remember from Nat's pitch while I was an apprentice train*ee*, and before I became a train*er*:

Mickey Mouse Park

Walt's first concept, which eventually evolved into Disneyland, was called Mickey Mouse park. It was to be located on a triangular section of studio property on Riverside Drive, right across from Forest Lawn Mortuary.

Enter Stanford Research

An architect friend of Walt's suggested that he retain Stanford Research to do a land feasibility study for his theme park idea. Nat said that Walt gave them two months to complete the study for a fee of $250.

Not Enough Land

The Stanford group determined that there was not enough land on the triangular lot for Walt's dream. Further, there was no space for parking, and the roads and freeways were not adequate to handle the estimated traffic increase.

Planned Freeways

Stanford Research had studied the freeways projected for the massive changes in southern California transportation. The as-yet-incomplete Santa Ana Freeway was designed to drop people off at the entrance of Disneyland.

Flat Land

Walt wanted flat land so he could create his own lakes, mountains, and rivers. He was creating a show, and what stage has mountains and valleys?

Not Near the Beach

It shouldn't be near the beach. His audience was mid-America, and he didn't want a beach crowd in bare feet and swimming trunks spoiling his dream.

The Price

Originally, the idea was to have free admission. Then, four months before opening, they decided to charge an admission price of 25 cents for adults and 15 cents for children, just to keep the undesirables out.

No Gum or Cotton Candy

Nat pointed out that Walt hated the usual amusement park dirt, and Disneyland would be *clean*—which ruled out selling gum or cotton candy.

I was shot full of luck. While my mind was as open as a child's, I was trained by three super salesmen: Walt Disney, C.V. Wood, and Nat Wyncoff.

Each in his own way created a feeling of excitement about the Disneyland Dream, although some of us really didn't understand it.

My orientation to Disneyland would not end on that day at the studio. After more than three decades, people still wonder why Walt hocked his life insurance to get a little more cash to build Disneyland. And Walt would explain:

> So I had a little dream for Disneyland adjoining the studio, but I couldn't get anybody to go in with me because we were going through the Depression. And whenever I'd go down and talk to my brother about it, why, he'd suddenly get busy with some figures, so, I mean, I didn't dare bring it up.

> But I kept working at it, and worked on it with my own money. Not the studio's money, but my own money. And eventually it evolved into what you see at Disneyland today. But it all started from a daddy with two daughters wondering where he could take them so he could have a little fun with them, too.

> It is something that will never be finished. Something that I can keep developing, keep plussing and adding to. It's *alive*. It will be a live breathing thing that will need change.

> A picture is one thing; once you wrap it up and turn it over to Technicolor, you're through. I can't change it. But I can change the park, because it is alive. That's why I wanted that park.

> I think what I want Disneyland to be most of all is a happy place—a place where adults and children can experience together some of the wonders of life, of adventure, and feel better because of it.

The Disneyland Castle

> I read in a magazine that the Neuschwanstein Castle in Bavaria was the model for "Disney's Fantasy Castle".

> I immediately sent a note to Dave Smith, the head of our Disney Archives and a fine person who will go into shock if he reads the errors in this story. His reply to my questions were:

> "No, Van, or at least only partially. The Disneyland Castle was a composite of many European castles, with the one you mentioned being studied."

> I might add that our castle, symbolizing "fantasy in any language", is almost as well recognized as Mickey Mouse.

Many years later, Wood and I were having drinks and dinner at the La Costa Resort in Carlsbad, California. As is always true when Disneyland people get together, we reminisced.

And Wood said, "It started with a buck."

I said, "How's that?"

"Well, when DISNEYLAND was established as a copyrighted name, I immediately rushed to the bank and made a deposit of ONE DOLLAR to make it legal."

Money was *really* tight in those days.

SEVEN

I See "The Site"

At the studio, key people were always going to or coming from "The Site".
Never Disneyland, always "The Site".

I felt the time had come for me to see "The Site".

First, I was just plain curious. And perhaps I just wanted to come back
to the studio and say, "I've just returned from 'The Site'."

But more important, I knew from experience that designers never allo-
cate space for training. I had to find myself some space.

I presented my curiosity and need to Fred Schumacher.

Fred arranged for me to be met by Earl Shelton, the "site coordinator".
He took Walt around in a jeep on his regular inspection trips. I headed
down the not-yet-completed Santa Ana Freeway to the boulevard stop at
Harbor and the construction entrance to "The Site".

I managed to find Earl in what they called the Administration Building—
two houses which had been put together for a useful purpose when others
were being destroyed by bulldozers.

I was to find out that Earl had a quiet sense of humor, a brilliant mind
behind the gruff exterior, and a memory like a computer.

Earl was one of Wood's boyhood friends who had escaped from Amarillo
to attend the University of Texas and then went on to became an Army
pilot in World War II. In the process he had lost any Texas accent he may
once have had, which didn't really matter because he didn't talk much.

I certainly need a guide. The site was an anthill of activity, if you accept
the theory that ants know what they are doing. Tractors, earth-moving
equipment, and craftsmen of all kinds were working against a deadline
six months away.

The rush of activity, confirmed by Earl, meant there was no place within
"The Site" where I could set up a training program. Earl understood and
steered the jeep to West Street, where the Disneyland Hotel was to be located.

All of the homes which were on the property we owned were named for
the former owners. Earl showed me an old, two-story home named the

Vandenburg House. As is the case with vacant homes, it was dirty, with lawns gone to weeds; but for me, it was a dream house.

In his quiet way, Earl said he thought we could use it. He worked without notes, but he always followed through. By the time I returned to the studio, he had called Wood, who approved this beach head on the perimeter of confusion.

I was happy with that important day's work, and I could now say with a bit of pride that I'd just returned from "The Site".

The Administration Building

Today we have a rather austere Administration Building with three floors, a basement, and even an elevator.

In 1955, the Administration Building was made from two old ranch homes placed together, one of which was once the home of Ron Dominguez, who went on to become vice president of Disneyland.

Walt's office had formerly between a bedroom. Adjacent to his office was another bedroom, which he sometimes used when he spent the night at "The Site".

Those old homes all had a second story and Wood's office was located upstairs.

Other people were in ex-dining room and ex-closets. There was only one bathroom in the entire facility.

EIGHT

Why Anaheim?

Until I visited "The Site", I'd never stopped in Anaheim. Raised in San Diego, Anaheim was a little town one drove *through*.

Of all the places Walt could have built his dream, why did he pick Anaheim? This is how he explained it.

> Well, you know this Disneyland concept kept growing and growing, and finally ended up where I felt like I needed two or three hundred acres. So I wanted it in the southern California area; it had certain things I needed, such as flat land where I could make my own hills. I had a survey group [Stanford] go out and hunt for areas that might be useful, and they finally came back with several different areas, and we settled on Anaheim.

> The price was right, but there was more to it than that, and that is Anaheim was sort of a growing area, and the freeway project was such that we could see eventually the freeways would hit Anaheim as sort of a hub, so that's how we selected Anaheim. In addition, "The City of Muscle", as Anaheim called itself, had a unique blend of city officials – young, dynamic managers as well as a few "good ol' boy" politicians. They *wanted* Disney and Disneyland in their community.

And Woody was the ideal Disney representative. He was young and charismatic, and he could charm farmers out of their orange groves with his Texas talk. I don't know, and I don't even want to know, about some of the ways borders were changed and people were persuaded to sell their land to Disney. The historical fact is that in a short time Walt had about 340 acres of land on which to build his dream, which would change Anaheim forever. The average price of land was about $4,500 per acre. Much of it would later sell for thousands per front foot.

It sounds as though Walt and the city slickers made a terrific deal, but at the time it was fair and square.

The citrus business was in a slump, and the Anaheim area was getting competition from other areas. For the farmers who were fighting for survival, $4,500 an acre was an attractive price. (Clearing away their orange trees after we bought the land was a major task. The trees which were to be saved were marked with large, red tags; those to be bulldozed had green ones. When a workman was seen cutting down the trees which were to be saved, it was found not to be his fault. He was just color blind.)

Walt's predictions about the city were absolutely on target. Anaheim has become a major leisure and entertainment center.

Walt sorely regretted that he didn't have enough money to buy the land surrounding his site, for he despised what the called the "cheap, Las Vegas appearance" of Harbor Boulevard.

Immediately after opening, the land value skyrocketed, and those who had property on the periphery tried to sell or lease their land at fantastic prices.

If you talk to any "old-timer" in Anaheim, or in any part of Orange County, you'll hear "what if" stories of the people who *should have bought* or who *should have held onto* land.

Art Linkletter, one of Hollywood's TV personalities, was rumored to be one of the wealthiest men and a canny land investor. His friend Walt tried to talk him into buying the acreage on Harbor Boulevard, but Art thought it was a bad investment. Now Art says, "Every time I walk there, my not buying it costs me about a million dollars a step."

••

Anaheim, Azusa, and Cucamonga

Once upon a time, young readers, there were no Sunday evening TV shows. There was no TV.

People across the country would wait for the Jack Benny radio show. Every Sunday the show would include a gag where a gravelly voiced train conductor would announce: "Now leaving for Anaheim, Azusa, and *Cuca*monga."

It was good for a laugh, even though people might not know they were real city names. I wonder what would have happened if Walt had selected *Cuca*monga as Disneyland's home?

••

NINE

I Hire a "Gofer"

*Gofer: A term used for a newly hired person who is
asked by superiors to "go for" this or "go for" that.*

My work load was building up. After seeing "The Site" and the abandoned home where we would do the training, I knew I needed some help...a gofer. Once again I appealed to Fred for help, since he received all job applications. He passed me an application, commenting: "This guy looked pretty good, but we can't reach him by phone."

I checked the application. Fortunately, I was familiar with the L.A. phone prefixes. (I should note that in those ancient times there were names in addition to numbers. In this case, Fred has been phoning PL, for Pleasant, when the applicant's number actually began PR, for Prospect.) I called the right number and made an appointment with a young man named Dick Nunis.

In came this six-foot, two-inches tall blond, aggressive, ex-football player. At the time I didn't know that he was a legend at USC, an Academic All-American because of his football record and a 3.6 grade-point average. I would have hired *anyone*, but I hired him in five minutes.

Although the interview was short, there were some aspects which I lived to regret. At that time, I was more prejudiced than I would become with the mellowness of age. Dick had dressed perfectly for a 21-year-old who was going on an interview – the USC graduate look. It included a pair of new suede shoes. Back then, I associated these with pimps, con men, and used car dealers. I asked him to never again wear those shoes to work around *me*.

He swears that I offered him $2.00 an hour, and that he received only $1.80. It's been an on-going debate for 30 years.

As I'll explain more thoroughly later in this book, Dick Nunis was to become a protégé of Walt Disney's, and eventually the president of Disneyland and Walt Disney World. More important, years later I would end up working for him as a staff assistant, which is the polite term for the more descriptive "gofer". So there is a moral to this story:

Be nice to your gofer; he may become your boss.

TEN

Goodbye Burbank, Hello Anaheim

My handbook and visual aids were nearly complete. I had collected every bit of Disney material I could borrow, beg, or steal. It was time to go where the action was getting frantic.

I had my last dinner at the Olive Branch bar and grill, and the next morning I drove down the still-not-completed Santa Ana Freeway to Anaheim, California...population 22,000.

Today, if you drive down West Street, you'll be on a busy, six-lane road crowded with motels and the massive towers of the Disneyland and Emerald hotels. When I drove there in 1955, it was a two-lane road bounded by orange trees and four remaining homes, including the abandoned Vandenburg house, our future training center.

I had told Dick to report to this dirty home, which hadn't been lived in for a year, in his working clothes, not the nice duds he'd worn for the interview. I'm getting a little bit ahead of my story, but 15 years later when he was responsible for opening Walt Disney World, some of us called him the "White Tornado". And, since I was mostly doing other things, he worked one of his first miracles by turning that old home into an attractive training center.

Since our new home was painted white, and since few of us foreigners could pronounce its German name, it soon became the "White House".

When Earl Shelton saw what we were doing, he managed to loan us some craftsmen. They painted the place inside and knocked out the wall between two bedrooms, giving us a training room into which we would later squeeze 40 people. We swept, dusted, and washed windows. The fresh paint and decorations made the place as attractive as possible, and transformed an Orange County home into something that had the firm imprint of DISNEY.

If you'll pardon a self-congratulation, I'll have to admit that scrounging that old home for training was a lot of good luck combined with pure genius.

Many of the people arriving later couldn't find a place to set up shop. We had space, and fortunately Dick proved to be as good a scrounger, liar, and thief as I was.

Within a few weeks we were to become a temporary home for the Safety Department, the Fire Department, the Medical Department, an extension of the Personnel Department, and the Wonderland Music Company, in addition to being a source of information for those who were confused by the hectic atmosphere at "The Site".

Dick was such a damned good worker that people wanted to borrow him, and I would loan him out if it seemed politically prudent.

I didn't plan it that way, but it helped us to become something more than a "Training Department", and Dick and I had a chance to find out how to move around and get things done in the pre-opening sea of confusion.

That Vandenburg house had been, truly, a home. Facing West Street were two porches—one for sitting or entering the living room, and one off the bedroom upstairs. There were five bedrooms. Every kid must have had his or her own little space.

The home, including a driveway and carport, was surrounded by fruit-bearing trees—not just orange trees, but lemon, avocado, peach, plum, and pomegranate trees. It was spacious, comfortable, and convenient. There was a cellar for food storage, an abandoned chicken coop, and a cage for rabbits.

Next door, separated from the Vandenburg house only by the trees, was the home of Mrs. Mohn. She had sold her land, but had a clause under which she could stay as long as she wanted. Her home was equally lovely, but still lived in. Her chickens knew no boundaries.

In the morning, before the day's rush began, I would come in and walk around the estate, enjoying the fragrance of orange blossoms. And frequently Mrs. Mohn would invite me in for morning coffee.

I fixed up a little office in what had once been a child's bedroom. It was a cozy haven in a sea of confusion. I could look across the upstairs porch to "The Site" and watch the work being done on West Street. At the end of a long day, I would bring in some beer or scotch...to preview progress or plan for the next day. It was a time that would now be called "happy hour".

For those who owned these ranches like the Vandenburg home, it must have been a perfect place to live, to raise a family. Although the Vandenburgs and others sold out for what was then a fair price, I wonder how they could find a lifestyle which could compare with what they left.

Those of us working on the Disneyland project felt that we were bringing "progress" to a farming community. And in the name of progress we replaced the fragrance of orange groves with the smell of smog, two-lane roads with freeways, and comfortable homes with motels, shopping centers, and fast food restaurants.

The White House served a useful purpose for at least two years. Eventually, what had been a warm and gracious home was torn down and replaced by the driving range for the Disneyland Hotel.

I was not around several years later when that old home was bulldozed down. I might have cried.

••

Ron Dominguez:
Our "Native Disneylander"

One of the pre-opening pioneers, who would say "Anaheim" when asked where he was born, had been raised on a ten-acre orange grove which would become the Rivers of America in Frontierland.

Ron Dominguez had begun doing ranch chores at about age six, and then worked in the groves while going to school. When Walt bought this critical ranch, Ron, only 18 years old, was one of the first natives, and one of a very few, who went to work at Disneyland.

Tall, good looking, and rugged, Ron might have been picked by Central Casting for the role on the Mike Fink Keel Boats—one of our most popular shows during the early days.

Those staged fights with an occasional dunking gained Ron more fame than the fact that he was working on the land of his own family's former orange groves.

As many of us did, Ron took the job as a temporary summer experience, but he became involved with the Disney dream...and stayed.

He worked on nearly every attraction in the park and finally realized his own dream—as executive vice president of Disneyland and the mayor of our community.

••

Our handbook was finally all pasted up and ready for printing. I thought I'd better check it out with Fred Schumacher, who would eventually pay the bill. I caught Fred at home, and he glanced at it. Actually, it was too late to make any major change. Fred was familiar with Disney copyright laws, and he suggested that I check it out with the Legal Department.

I was busy and so I asked Dick to take it to there for me. He came back in a state of minor shock. (I should mention that "Circle C" is the copyright symbol and "WDP" stands for Walt Disney Productions.) "This guy," Dick told me, "says we've got to have a Circle C, WDP on every damned illustration." To make his point, the lawyer had pounded on the desk every time he intoned those precious words: Circle C, WDP...Circle C, WDP...Circle C, WDP...

Dick learned his lesson as well and has caught me more than once when I've forgotten that legalistic "bug".

ELEVEN

"You'll Create Happiness"

I believe entertainment usually fills some vital need and normal curiosity for every man, woman, and child who needs it.

— Walt Disney

Thursday, May 26, 1955, was a historic day for me and my Disneyland career.

It was the morning for me to present the orientation program for the people who would operate Disneyland on opening day, July 17. Assembled in a training program which had been converted from two upstairs bedroom was a jury of executives who could hang me at sunset.

We had "Disneyized" that old White House in every way we could. This was homey...not sanitized.

Walt's brother Roy Disney was the brilliant financial genius who raised the money for Walt's dreams. And he would be the final judge for this training program for a theme park.

He was right there in the front row, seated next to the vice president of the Bank of America and key executives from Eastman Kodak, Swift and Company, and others.

Wood was there, sitting next to Card Walker, vice president of Disney Marketing, and Donn Tatum, vice president for Legal Affairs.

In addition, I'd made certain I had some supporting friends in the group. I could count on Jack Sayers, Fred Schumacher, and Dorothy Manes to nod, smile, or laugh at the right points.

And Dick was there to make it a two-man show. Although he was young, he had a personality that exuded confidence.

Our visual aids were primitive by modern standards. We had beautiful cards which were about two by four feet in size. We had one carousel slide projector, and I had a large flannel board which was a piece of felt stapled to a large board. We used little pie-shaped cards with a bit of Velcro on the back to make them stick to the flannel.

To loosen up the group—and me, too—I asked everyone to stand up, tell their names, and where they were born. It was fun because no one in the group had been born in Anaheim and not many were native Californians, either. Roy Disney was a good participant and made it easy for the other top executives. Dick's birthplace of Cedartown, Georgia, got a laugh, and when Jack Sayers mentioned his birthplace of Fairbanks, Alaska, people turned around to see if he was an Eskimo.

After the group relaxed a bit, I introduced Dick who gave a slide presentation of an artist's renderings of what Disneyland would be. He may have been worried along with me, but it didn't show. He brought these slides to life, and made a confident, motivational presentation. I was proud of him.

After Dick wound up his pitch, I moved over to my flannel board to describe the team work involved in the existing Disney enterprises of movies, TV, comic books, and merchandise, as well as pointing out the record number of Oscar awards and other Disney milestones and pioneering landmarks. Each of these activities was depicted on a round visual aid on round cardboard which looked like pie plates.

I gave the group a stand-up break and then prepared to present what would become forever Disneyland's basic policy for serving those who would come to Walt's dream park. I was worried more about this presentation than any I'd ever done before, or since, and the fear was justified.

In this group were men who had invested their careers and millions of dollars in what the experts predicted would be a financial failure. Money was not just a problem—it was a constant crisis.

I presented the first of our cards which depicted a dream castle with blocks showing Disney traditions of Art, Music, Adventure, and Fantasy. And then I pointed out that the entire history of Walt's life had been to entertain and educate—a tradition of family entertainment. And now, as Walt's twenty-year dream was to open in a few weeks, we at Disneyland were going to follow that tradition. And the theme of our joint effort would be: WE'LL CREATE HAPPINESS.

It was a risky approach, but that group of executives bought the idea. The thousands of people whom we would train bought the concept. Most important, Walt liked it. We still use the theme more than 30 years later. It is important enough in my history, and the history of the company, to deserve the background for the approach.

We have used this Walt Disney quote many times, and it expresses the challenge we faced in creating that pioneering program:

> You can dream, create, and build the most wonderful place in the world, but it still take people to operate it.

Our challenge, for the first time, was to train people who could produce the dream. There were no precedents, no programs which we could copy. That was fortunate. I was forced to come up with new concepts.

We had one policy direct from Walt. He hated with a passion the dirt and sloppy service he had researched in his trips to amusement parks.

Previously, Walt had created his movies, which were distributed to theater operators. If there was gum on the seats, springs popping out to tear clothes, or bad popcorn, the *theater* got the blame, not Walt Disney.

But now each of us was a direct representative of the entire Disney organization. And we had our own special way of operating a dream and creating happiness for a new Disney audience.

Before that presentation, I had found that most people want to be involved in something greater than just being paid for a job. My basic story is about the two men laying bricks. When asked what he is doing, one may says, "I'm laying bricks." The other man performing the same task says, "I'm building a cathedral."

At Disneyland, I wanted people to feel they were involved in something more important than parking cars, serving food, or sweeping up popcorn. I want them to feel they were *creating happiness for others.*

You may be interested in the cards we used for the remainder of that historic program:

It All Started with a Mouse
Jack Sayers came up with the idea that everything that Disney had done actually started with a mouse named Mickey. We still use that thought.

The Magic Mirror of Your Smile
To explain the importance of a smile, Dick came up with the idea that a smile is a "magic mirror" helping to create smiles from others.

"It's Been My Pleasure"
In addition to a "friendly smile", we sold the importance of "smiling phrases". Dorothy Manes came up with a response for when *we* are thanked: "it's been my pleasure". The phrase was new to me, but I've used it thousands of times since then.

We Don't Have "Customers"...We Serve "Guests"
We *invite* people to visit Disneyland. Therefore, we treat them as guests.

We Are "Hosts" and "Hostesses"
Since we are entertaining guests, we were all "hosts" and "hostesses", regardless of our job title or function.

No Such Thing as a "Dumb" Question
Although we knew we'd get a lot of crazy questions, we should treat every question with respect, and answer it graciously, hundreds of times a day.

Everyone's a V.I.P.

This was an anti-prejudice point. The guests pay us. We treat everyone, regardless of race, creed, color, or political views, with the V.I.P. treatment.

The Disneyland Look

Here we could say we were all part of a show, and that appearance and costuming were essential to a "good show". At that time, I had no worry about the young men we hired. They were all as clean as Tab Hunter or the Beaver. The problem, we would soon find, was with our hostesses who at the time presented themselves in outlandish, red-dyed, beehive hair styles.

Disneyland Taboos

At the time, and even now, company training programs start out with the "thou shalt nots"—all negatives. We told people they were the best and softened the negatives by calling them "taboos".

We Work While Others Play

Here we warned people of the hard fact that working at Disneyland was not a 9-5, Monday-Friday, kind of job.

The pitch wound up with the essential need for team work between everyone, including all lessees. And together we would be pioneers in one of the great dreams in Disney's history.

At the end of program, we received a round of applause. Roy Disney came up to thank both Dick and me. He had a good sense of humor and said, "Now, Van, we are going to create a lot of happiness, but we're also going to have to make money to get Walt's life insurance out of hock. In fact, I'm leaving right now to borrow some more money to meet the payroll."

Wood shook my hand and breathed a sigh of relief. After all, he had recommended me for the job. But his feeling of relief couldn't have been as great as mine.

Dick had been sweating it out right along with me. We had been approved of by the jury of our peers. We both had others things to do, but we met at my little room in the White House. he had a drink, then left, and I sat there with some scotch, smelling the fragrance of the orange trees and watching Mrs. Mohn's chickens scratch for their evening meal.

In selling others on the importance of creating happiness, I think I had convinced *myself.*

TWELVE

From Happiness To Highways

After that historical day—at least it was for me—we had a chance to try out the program on supervisors and newly hired people. They also responded well to this motivational approach.

But before I had a chance to rest on my laurels, I got a call from Wood who told me to get myself over to his office "right NOW!"

As usual, his office was crowded, but he accosted me as soon as I came in.

"Van, that training program is off the ground, and Dick can handle it. But unless we can move people in and out, we're in deep trouble. You're going to learn about roads and highways around here."

In a room adjacent to Wood's office, perhaps formerly a closet in the Dominguez home, were some Stanford Research people around a desk on top of which was a state-of-the-art mechanical adding machine. Woody took me aside to introduce me to Jim Thompson, saying: "This man knows more about traffic projections than *anybody*, and he'll educate you.

He *did* educate me, and we became friends.

Jim was a brilliant statistician, or "numbers man", as Wood described him. He had been part of the Stanford Research team that made all the original traffic predictions.

Wood's assessment of the potential traffic crisis was not exaggerated. It was legitimate panic time, and it was only 50 days till opening.

At that time, there was *no* San Diego Freeway, *no* Garden Grove Freeway, *no* Riverside Freeway, *no* Pomona Freeway. For modern transportation, there was an uncompleted Santa Ana Freeway, and that was it.

Traffic—getting people *to* and *from* Disneyland—would prove to be a major problem. If it had not been for local heroes of all involved government groups, Disneyland's opening might have been a disaster.

When it came to training and human relations, I knew my business. When it came to roads, highways, and traffic, my experience was limited to driving a car. And now I was to become an instant expert. I was a city fellow who was going to seek help from some small-town country hicks.

I visualized meeting people who wore high, black shoes, starched collars, and galluses (suspenders). I expected people who didn't drink, smoke, or swear, and who spent all day Sunday in church. I was wrong. I was about to meet a much more sophisticated group of people than I expected, and as dedicated as one could find anywhere in city, county, and state government.

We like to talk about "dreamers" and "doers". And now, totally involved in Walt's dream, was a group of men who were to work together to create some miracles in traffic coordination.

A committee was formed. It included Keith Murdoch, Anaheim's City Manager; Mark Stephenson, Chief of Police; Herb Null, Captain of the Highway Patrol; Fran Cheathan of the Orange County Road Department; Jim Thompson; and myself.

They deserve a place in the annals of pre-opening Disneyland history.

TPD

I found that these initials (TPD) stood for Theoretical Peak Day. This was a basic statistic on which much of Disneyland's land planning was based. Here is its theoretical base.

43,700 people would enter the park at about 8am, and another 43,700 would enter and stay until 8pm. On a peak day, Disneyland theoretically would receive 87,400 people.

As an example, the TPD was used for acquiring land for parking. It was projected that 93 percent of our guests would come by car. Each car would have 3.7 occupants. As a result, 112 acres of parking would be required.

Although operations would change radically, these statistics were amazingly accurate. It was 18 years before we first had to close the parking lot due to an overabundance of guests. And, on August 16, 1969, we first hit our single-day record of 82,516 visitors.

By the authority I give myself for writing this history, I'll give myself credit for completing the Harbor off-ramp two days before opening. Cars would come down the freeway and hit a boulevard stop. Wood warned us, "Without that off-ramp, traffic will be backed up to San Francisco!"

The problem was that the contractor's agreement stipulated that no overtime be paid by the state. I went to meet the superintendent of the job.

Fortunately, he was a young guy who understood our problem. Without any paperwork, except Wood's okay, I said we'd pay for any overtime involved. And I threw in a lunch if they could complete it before opening day. That off-ramp was finished two days before opening. A crisis had been averted. We celebrated over lunch and cocktails. I got my off-ramp... and a hangover.

Everyone on our traffic team knew more about everything than I ever would. I did, however, have special advantages. A gold parking pass for my car gained me admittance anywhere in the park. And, although I never bribed anyone, I had an unlimited expense account and access to preview day passes which were better than gold.

Budgets, forms, procedures? I can't remember any. We got the job done, and that was what mattered.

THIRTEEN

A Shotgun Marriage With 29 Unions

Although I was worrying about roads, highways, the Harbor off-ramp, training, and a few other things, I managed to become partially involved in another major crisis: union negotiations.

We were now up to the critical days of June, but way back in January, Fred Schumacher had worried about the unions who wanted to organize Disneyland. After one frustrating meeting, Fred complained, "Van, I'm trying to get Woody to face up to the union situation, but he insists that we aren't going to *have* any union!"

Walt still carried the scars of a bitter strike at the studio, and he was probably quite willing to accept this wishful thinking on Wood's part. Since Disneyland was a totally new concept of entertainment, there was a certain logic in starting out with no unions. But it was not to be. Logic had nothing to do with the realities:

- All of the pre-publicity had excited the union leaders as well as the public. Here, the unions felt, was a chance to participate in Walt's dream.

- The construction unions had us over the barrel. Their members were working, and working hard, to meet the deadline. They let us know that if they didn't have a contract, we couldn't open.

- Although the *Mark Twain* riverboat would operate on a guide rail, the inland boatmen wanted jurisdiction over these operators at the same rates that were paid to those guiding ships to Catalina Island.

- The American Guild of Variety Artists (AGVA) wanted jurisdiction over those who would operate the Jungle Cruise boats, along with the rates paid to professional show people.

In addition to Wood and Fred Schumacher, there were two other key personalities who were intimately involved in this unusual negotiation which would establish precedents for Disneyland's future human relations policies.

Fred Newcombe was Disneyland's personnel director. He was a graduate of Stanford University and had ended up in personnel and labor relations in various aircraft industries. He was a quiet, intelligent man who would type out complex policies and agreements on his old typewriter. And he was trusted by both union and company people.

Ben Nathenson was a labor consultant from Los Angeles. He was very intense, always peering through his horn-rimmed glasses. He was always on a diet, and in one of those strange flashes of memory, I can remember his feeling guilty about eating a cracker...25 calories.

I had worked with Ben when I was handling labor relations for a Los Angeles company. While working within the field, I had discovered that labor relations was the toughest aspect of human relations. But here I was an observer, and one day at lunch Ben used me as a sounding board for his frustrations.

"Van," he said, "this is the toughest consulting job I've ever had. We're over the barrel. We're still suffering from that plumber's strike. If the construction unions were to walk out for even two days, we'd never get this place opened."

I wasn't allowed to sit in on these meetings, but I found a way to be kept up to date. I would find out from the two Freds and Ben how things were going. And during the final sessions they'd sometimes make me pay for my curiosity by sending me out to fetch sandwiches.

The agreement which was reached was as unique as Disneyland itself. We ended up with a contract which included 29 unions. One of them— for the person who shod horses—had only a single member. There were established unions for most of the people, but it was difficult to know how to categorize someone who would guide a Jungle Cruise boat in Anaheim.

This problem was settled with the understanding that if our young ride operators wanted a union, we would recommend the Teamsters. If they didn't *want* to join any union, we couldn't force them to sign up. However, most who wanted a job at the park felt it was the prudent thing to do. With various modifications, this marriage of necessity (a necessity for management) has held together for more than 35 years.

When the full impact of the negotiations was understood, Walt was mad as hell. Fortunately, Ben Nathenson had been the consultant whose recommendations had been accepted. It's my theory that when there's a new development where mistakes, and lots of them, are to be expected, one person should be hired as a corporate scapegoat—the mistake maker. Ben, friendly Ben, filled that role. His agreement was cancelled. His was the head that rolled. It had been an interesting drama to watch, especially since I didn't have to take any of the heat.

FOURTEEN

Deadline Days

Nobody had been loafing.

We had all been working seven-day weeks. And yet when July 1 rolled around, the date had an impact.

This was the month when we would be opening, and that meant there were only 16 days before dedication.

The original $4 million estimate for Disneyland had ballooned to $17 million. Never before had a show opening on Broadway, or anywhere, cost that much. And we couldn't take this show to Boston to try it out first and make any needed changes.

In 16 days, only 384 hours, Walt would be presenting his dream to about 90 million TV viewers and a live audience of celebrities and critics.

Who gave a damn about the Fourth of July? Well, for some it was an overtime day, but for most of us it was a precious day for planning. These weren't *bad* days. They were exciting and challenging.

Today in Anaheim there are about a dozen bars within walking distance of Disneyland. It was different in 1955. There was only one bar and restaurant (incorrectly called the *Water* Wheel) which was modern. At the end of a long day, this became an after-work meeting place. Over drinks there was always only *one* topic of discussion. You guessed it. Disneyland.

Even if I were that type of person, I would have been too tired to jot down "Dear Diary" notes before going to bed. But some things come to mind as I recall those precious 16 days before opening. I can't remember any sequence. To explain those days is like looking into a kaleidoscope. Turn it this way or that and there's a myriad of individual stories. I can jump-start my memory and come up with some which I'll include here.

Walt's Bicycle

A bicycle was the preferred means of getting around "The Site". Unfortunately, our bikes had a habit of breaking down. Back then, things didn't get done by procedure. We used a certain amount of guilt, bluff, friends, grease, and lies. One trick was to use Walt's name. For example, "Please repair Walt's bike" would get immediate action—and who was to know that Walt never rode a bike?

Although he didn't ride a bicycle, Walt managed to amaze me by the way he'd get around "The Site" by walking. One day I saw Walt at one end of the park to-be. I was driving. But, by the time I got to the other side of the park, he was already there. I guess it was due to his days on the farm and delivering papers, because he could cover a lot of distance on foot, without seeming to be in a hurry.

The Moving Bandstand

One Sunday, I brought my daughter to "The Site" while I finished up some work. We walked down the incomplete Main Street. A bandstand was located at the center of Town Square where the flagpole now stands.

Walt was standing there just looking at it. At the risk of interrupting his thoughts, I introduced my daughter. He was gracious, as he always was to children, but definitely preoccupied. Sort of talking to himself, but also to us, he said, "There's something damned wrong with the location of that bandstand." Leaving him alone with his thoughts, my daughter and I left.

The next morning I was on Main Street and saw the bandstand being moved to where Carnation Gardens now stands. That bandstand never did find a proper home, although it was moved several times before and after opening. I've heard it is now located in a nursery in Newport Beach.

The "Horse People"

My only failure in getting people to attend orientation was with the men who would operate our horse-drawn vehicles and drive the mule pack. I finally cornered Owen Pope, the crusty and independent man who managed what we called the Pony Farm. "Van," he said, "you deal with *people* people. Out here, we are *horse* people." But he did manage to send Day Sechler, his foreman, to orientation. Owen conducted his own orientation program...for the horses. He worried that they might "spook" with the sounds and sights of the crowds, so he produced a tape of yelling kids, arcade noises, and the bark of guns in the shooting gallery. He played it for the horses before opening, and that program was effective.

The Pony Farm was also the home of our mule pack. The Property Control people could hardly put an identification tag on a mule, but the four-legged creatures did require names. Lucy Cottom of Finance came up with a name for each mule. She started with "Lucy Mule" and continued with the names of the people who worked with her.

Golden Time

The final days weren't all bad for the union construction workers and others who punched the time clock. They were earning more than mere "overtime". They would get extra pay for time worked over 40 hours...for the sixth day and the seventh day. After a number of hours and days, it added up to what is called "Golden Time". For some, this would amount to more than $1,000 a week, in 1955 dollars—about five times what I was getting.

In fact, Dick was punching the time clock and giving me a timecard to sign, which I never even looked at. After 30 years, when we have a few drinks, he still complains about my offering him $2.00 an hour and giving him only $1.80. And because he was on the clock, I accuse him of having made much more than my $200 a week flat fee. To this date, he never has denied making more than I did way back in 1955, but he still bitches about that 20 cents.

Sleeping on the Job

Dave Bartchard was hired as a truck driver in 1954. "When I started to work here," he said, "Main Street was nothing but 2x4 stakes and chalk marks. Frequently, Walt would hitch a ride with me. Once he told me how he drove an ambulance for the Red Cross in after World War I. He always treated a man like a man. The last two months before opening I was on the job 24 hours a day. I'd sleep in my truck, and I only went home on Sundays.

Harley's Tent

For months, the construction crew had been eating from potable food trucks referred to as "roach coaches". Harley, one of the food providers, added a bit of style to this food service. He got approval to set up a permanent tent. "Harley's Tent" was our cafeteria for pre-opening and through the following year. It was a major social center. Walt would plop down and eat a hot dog with anyone who was there. We guessed that when Harley left, he was a rich man. Not only did he handle the football and baseball pools, but he also ran a loan service. You could borrow five bucks until payday and pay back six...good interest for a one-week loan.

Stage Fights

During the final days, there was a continuing fight between the construction crew and the TV crew. TV crews would fight to lay cable and rehearse participants for the show. Then, they would be chased off by the construction crew, who had *their* deadlines.

About two days before opening, Tommy Walker informed us that the TV director would not be directing the program on opening day. The pressure had taken its toll. He had had a heart attack, perhaps because he'd never been required to produce a show under these extreme circumstances. The show went on, and the director recovered sufficiently to watch it on TV from his bed in a local hospital.

A Pressure Release in the Peltzer House

A family named Peltzer had, before selling out, lived in another old home right where the north end of the parking lot is now. It was used as an office by the Duning Construction Company.

It had to be torn down before the grading and surfacing of the parking lot could begin. Rather than simply using a bulldozer, somebody suggested that we have a house-wrecking party. Woody approved, with the thought that it might be a good way to release some tensions before the final pre-opening push.

Somebody provided liquor. How and why nobody was hurt amazes me. There were windows broken, chandeliers pulled down, stairways wrecked, walls hacked at, and plumbing torn out.

I helped our safety engineer keep a semblance of order, and when the crowd had thinned out, we left to have another drink in quieter, and safer, surroundings. Eventually, somebody dropped a match and the fire department was called.

The last of the old homes on "The Site" was now gone. The next day parking lot construction began. We newcomers—the carpet-baggers—and the Texans didn't realize the significance of this destruction of the last of the old homes. It was the end of an era, and Anaheim would never be that quiet, sleepy little town again.

Now it was back to the serious and tension-filled days which lay ahead.

Shorty Harrington

Shorty was an unsung hero during the deadline days, although his methods were not the kind one would sing about. In one case, he ended an argument with the foreman of a cement-laying crew with a single punch which flattened the man, who had been loafing on the job.

When Herb Null came to the White House to set up the Highway Patrol communications system, he asked a good question: "How many people will be here on opening day?" I didn't know. I asked Fred and Wood and everyone else who should know. Confused answers. The problem was that this was a special invitation affair. And distribution of the passes had been loose, very loose.

Finally, after checking every other source, I got together with our printer. Our best figures indicated that we had given out nearly 15,000 passes. In addition, we had given 6,000 passes to the families of the construction crew. We had an emergency meeting and decided that the construction workers' passes couldn't be used until the week after opening.

Opening day more than exhausted the capacity of the park and the facilities. If the additional 6,000 construction folks had also come, it probably would have been a *major* disaster.

I've always wondered how we ended up with the address of 1313 Harbor Boulevard. I heard recently that because it was the 1300 block, the city planner who was given the task of putting a number to Walt's dream simply repeated the first two digits, and that was that.

However, I'm convinced that Walt—always fighting tradition—felt that "13" was a *lucky* number and selected that address personally.

It was also the license plate for Donald Duck's car, and July 13 was the date of Walt's marriage to Lillian Bounds. It was also the day in 1955 he celebrated their 30th wedding anniversary with a huge party at Disneyland. The invitation was a mixture of good taste and humor:

Where: Disneyland...where there's plenty of room.

When: Wednesday, July 13, 1955, at 6:00 in the afternoon.

Why: Because we've been married 30 years.

How: By cruising down the Mississippi on the Mark Twain's maiden voyage, followed by dinner at Slue-foot Sue's Golden Horseshoe!

Hope you can make it...we especially want you. And, by the way, no gifts please...we have everything, including a grandson!

Lilly and Walt

Perhaps Walt knew that at this party he'd find out any major weaknesses before the Big Day.

It would be the first time for us to actually feed people, and it was a major challenge for the maiden voyage of the *Mark Twain* and the premiere of the Golden Horseshoe Revue shows.

Since I was worrying about that Harbor Boulevard off-ramp and many other things, I didn't attend, but I heard about the party from others.

"I started out the day doing orientation," remembers Dick Nunis. "Then, I had to change the room to make space for cots for the Highway Patrol unit. I helped schedule physical examinations, then ran errands for the safety engineer while following up on signs for traffic control.

"After a full day, I went to 'The Site' to don a Security costume to help direct the guests. And then I changed again to act as bartender on the *Mark Twain*. Finally, at about two in the morning, I cleaned up the *Mark* and made sure that the liquor was properly secured. I was back at the White House at six the next morning."

"I was out at the Main Gate" waiting with Walt for the invited guests," said Jack Sayers. "By six o'clock, nobody had shown up. The busses and cars had been caught in traffic.

"Walt was not a patient man. We paced and smoked together, and he kept asking me, 'Where are they?' I think he blamed *me* for the fact that everyone was late. Finally, the guests began to arrive. Walt quit pacing and greeted each guest by name."

In her book *My Dad, Walt Disney*, Walt's daughter Diane tells her remembrance of the end of the evening. Seeing that Walt was bone-tired, and elated, Diane asked her father:

Daddy, can I drive you home? He said, "Well, sure, honey. No problem at all." He just climbed in the back of the car. He had a map of Disneyland, and he rolled it up and tooted in my ear as with a toy trumpet. Before I knew it, all was silent. I looked around and there he was, asleep with his arms folded around the map like a boy with a toy trumpet, sound asleep. I knew he didn't have too much to drink, because the next morning he didn't have a hangover. He bounded out of the house at 7:30am and headed for Disneyland again.

Walt wasn't the only one back at the park at 7:30am. Many had been working all night, and the rest of us were there for the final countdown.

There were now only three days...72 hours...until the night before the opening.

FIFTEEN

'Twas the Night Before Opening

It was the night before opening, and you could feel the tension...for good reason.

This was no play you could try out in Boston before taking it to New York, no movie you could show in Azusa before releasing it nationally. Here we were opening a dream which many predicted would fail. This show was planted – in brick, mortar, electrical lines, and plumbing systems.

Not only was Walt's reputation riding on this revolutionary concept, he had hocked his life insurance and the price tag was now more than $17 million, which would probably be more than 170 million modern bucks.

Assembled for this once-in-a-lifetime event was as diverse a group as had ever been assembled for a single goal. Representatives from the City of Anaheim, Orange County, the State of California, the Marines, neighboring communities, and of course, all of our Disney people, the entertainers, and the TV crews.

I was all over the place, and I can remember the day and the evening as in little snapshots – some of which are clear and others blurred.

At the White House

The California Highway Patrol were set up in the old training room where they could nap or relax between shifts.

Dorothy Manes had arranged to feed the Boy Scouts, Girl Scouts, and school bands who would play a part in the ceremonies. To add to the general confusion, we were still using the White House to sign up some last-minute hosts and hostesses who would report for duty after having been given minimal orientation and training under the orange trees. Dick was coordinating the confusion in an adept way in what was a key outpost for the next day.

Walt's Uncle – To the Opening on Time

Walt's uncle Robert Disney was scheduled to give the invocation at the ceremonies. He was due to fly in on opening day and be driven to Anaheim. We worried that he would get tied up in traffic and not make it to the park in time The captain of the Anaheim Police Department was an enthusiastic participant in the preparations and was undaunted by this possible problem.

"Don't you worry, Van," he said. "I'll get him there if I have to bring him on my motorcycle." That extreme measure wasn't necessary, however; he arrived by car with time to spare.

Some Illegal Directional Signs

For anyone who didn't live in the area, just *finding* the entrance to Disneyland would be difficult. The problem was that there were many laws in Anaheim regarding signs and where they could be placed. We had arranged for signs to be placed by some gas stations, but at most corners they would be illegal. The city and the county were willing to work with us to handle the anticipated problem. We arranged for the signs to be made. Then, on the day before opening, we planted them, many illegally, where they were needed. In some cases, a few years passed before we were found out, but, by that time, we had some legal directional signs.

White Lines on Harbor Boulevard

Harbor Boulevard had been newly resurfaced, and one of my late evening duties was to work with county personnel to paint stripes down the middle of the street.

And Beer on West Street

On West Street, men were still finishing the curbing. Although they were on overtime, they were talking about leaving. I loaded my car with beer and, with the cold brew, motivated them to keep working.

Meanwhile...Inside "The Site"

Tommy Walker and Jack Sayers had made a deal with the construction crew that last night before opening. Tommy and Jack could have the park to set up and rehearse the TV show until 6 pm, and then the construction crew could come in to pour asphalt and add a few finishing touches. I didn't see Walt on that day before opening, but Jack said "just about everyone was worried except Walt. He seemed to love the excitement...and his calm rubbed off on all of us."

The Final Touches

All that night work would progress. Grass was being...not grown, but rolled out where needed. Asphalt was being poured, and a thousand details were being checked.

Since I was not a plumber or a painter, I met with Dick and the Highway Patrol group for a few beers, and then at midnight headed home.

I rolled and tossed until about four o'clock the next morning, and was back at the White House at six for what was, for me and many others, a historic event.

SIXTEEN

"The Site" Becomes "Disneyland, U.S.A.

At about 7 am on the morning of July 17, 1955, Jim Thompson, Dick, and I were having coffee with members of our special Highway Patrol unit before they headed out for their assignments.

The day had turned out hot and sultry, but clear. The Goodyear Blimp, stationed there for the event, was getting ready to hover over us for the opening. Herb Null, Captain of the Highway Patrol, arrived with Mark Stephenson, Police Chief of Anaheim, and we all boarded the blimp to check the Santa Ana Freeway and surrounding area.

Where was all the traffic? The area was deserted. We had forgotten that people were either at church or asleep.

But it was the quiet before the storm. Soon they woke up and headed for what was no longer "The Site" but Disneyland Park.

July 17 was billed as a "preview" for dignitaries and members of the press. We anticipated a small group which would be personally greeted by Walt Disney. I don't think even Walt expected a *mob*.

Although we had postponed the use of the 6,000 passes for construction personnel and their families, there were still several thousand more guests than anyone had expected. Our official records indicate that there were 28,154 guests in the park that day, and I'm not one to tamper with somebody's estimates.

However, *no one* who was there can confirm that number. We had special little machines to keep track of our attendance, but nobody remembered to turn them on that day. And with the capacity we had at the time, 28,000 would have created a riot, instead of just pandemonium.

Jim Thompson and I had it relatively easy with the traffic situation. After all, we had the trained, enthusiastic men of the Anaheim Police Department and our own special unit of the California Highway Patrol keeping things in hand.

All that day, and into the night, Jim and I performed gofer duties for our traffic men and handled emergencies, such as finding out where the Boy Scouts were supposed to report for duty. During a small break in the string of frequent crises, I suggested that we sneak back to the White House to see some of the TV program. Jim talked me out of that idea with a comment which summed up our feelings about that day: "What...and miss all this fun?"

It would 10 years before I had a chance to see a tape of that TV program, which preserved for all time the confusion of opening day.

Fifteen years later, we formed a club of veterans who were present and working at opening, called Club 55. Fortunately, we have a written record of notes from some of those who were in the park on that historic day.

The Jungle Cruise was the most popular attraction at the preview and during opening day. Attractions Host Pete Crimmings commented, "We didn't have megaphones for the narration, and we dreamed up most of it ourselves. Unfortunately, there were times when the hippos didn't hop as they were supposed to, and we had to ad lib a lot. They were were busy days. One guy had a record of 97 trips without a break."

Carpenter Scotty Cribbes was walking down Main Street early in the morning with a cup of coffee in each hand. He remembered: "Walt stopped me, and I thought I was going to be fired, but he just wanted to know where HE could get a cup. I gave him the cup I was taking to a friend, and Walt appreciated it with a big 'Thanks!'"

Ray Schwartz worked all night before the opening. He recalls Walt dropping by in Fantasyland. "He joked about it," Ray said, "but he told us, 'My life insurance money is paying for painting that Carousel.'"

Dick Nunis remembers seeing some of our well-dressed dignitaries stepping on wet asphalt while wearing high heels. Some proceeded in bare feet, and others contributed to the thousands of complaints we would receive.

Joyce Berlanger was working at the Main Gate, near the spot where Ronald Reagan was hosting the TV show. "Every time I looked around," Joyce said, "Ronald Reagan was taking his *contacts* out."

Rima Bruce was a secretary for the Foods Division. "Nobody knew their way around the park," she remembered. "It took an hour to get from Personnel to my job location. Then, we turned our office over to the press and went out to see that action. The only word for it was 'bedlam'."

Since there was a possibility that I would help direct traffic, my Highway Patrol friends gave me a valuable lesson. When cars were jammed up and lost, there was one standard answer to any request for directions. If drivers asked how to get out of Disneyland to San Diego, Los Angeles, or anywhere, the stock answer was "straight ahead". This way there would be no delay. And the drivers would eventually find their way home.

Most of the day, I was outside the park on traffic detail, but I did go inside to check on things.

I ran into Wood at the entrance to the Administration Building. This usually cool, calm, and collected man was out of character.

We had forgotten to lock the doors to Sleeping Beauty Castle. Internally, it was nothing but an incomplete shell. "Van," he yelled, "there are people up in that castle! Get them out before they kill themselves!" Sure enough, there were some people at the top of the castle enjoying the show. They had found an open door and climbed up on the construction platform. Larry Tryon, our finance director, stood guard at one door while we helped the people down from their precarious perch before they killed themselves.

Two facilities are just as essential to dignitaries as they are to any other humans: rest rooms and drinking fountains. And here we had big trouble.

We might have survived the construction delay caused by the rainiest spring in a decade if it had not been for a plumber's strike two months before opening. When the strike was settled, we were told we could have *either* rest rooms *or* drinking fountains by opening day, but not both.

We chose the rest rooms, and instead of drinking fountains we had young men carrying in water on their backs in our own version of Gunga Din. We were accused of not having drinking fountains so that our guests would have to buy Coca-Cola and Pepsi.

The number of rest rooms was totally inadequate. And they were difficult to find. Walt didn't want big signs saying MEN and WOMEN in our theme stages. So, in Fantasyland, they were called PRINCE and PRINCESS. Some of the guests thought they were attractions.

There were, of course, long lines at every attraction, but to our amazement, the longest line in the park was for the women's rest room on Main Street.

The White House resembled a Red Cross emergency tent that day.

The California Highway Patrol men came and went, and the local police used it as a sub-station to check traffic problems in the area.

Jim and I, with the help of the CHP, were able to make regular runs to the Water Wheel to get fried chicken and hamburgers for our patrol, and for the lost stragglers.

Finally, close to midnight, all the Boy Scouts and Girl Scouts had been picked up. The Highway Patrol had helped drivers of cars find their way out of the area, and were ready to sack out on their cots.

A few of us gathered to share the day's experiences and have some cold beer, but we were all a bit too tired to spend much time celebrating. After all, we had to be back at the crack of dawn to regroup for another critical day.

SEVENTEEN

"God Bless 'Em, Let 'Em Pee!"

The park preview day on July 17 had been *free* for our guests. The cash was flowing one way: OUT. And now we were to face Monday, July 18. Would people *pay* to share Walt Disney's dream?

Thirteen years later, I was the emcee for our annual reunion party of 1955 pioneers. To liven things up, I asked people to tell their favorite opening day stories. Roy Disney was our key speaker, seated at the head table with his wife, Edna.

He told us that as the one responsible for financing Disneyland, he had not been so confident as his brother Walt. He pointed out how the studio's every dollar was tied up in the Disneyland dream. What if we opened the gates and nobody came?

Roy had a glint in his eye, and Edna had that worried look that wives sometimes have when they don't know what their husbands are going to say.

The final words of Roy's speech were something like this:

> Well, on that day I left the studio and headed down the Santa Ana Freeway. I was worried. After getting out of Los Angeles, the traffic began to get heavy. It could have been people going to the beach.
>
> Because the freeway was not completed, it was stop and go most of the way. It must have taken more than an hour to finally get to the Disneyland parking lot, which was jammed. A young man working there recognized me and came up in a bit of a panic. He wasn't familiar with our first-name policy.

> "Mr. Disney," he said, "people have been stalled on the freeway getting into our parking lot. Children are peeing all over the lot."

> I looked around at all of these people who were coming here to pay to get in. With a great sense of relief, I said: "God bless 'em, let 'em pee!"

Walt Disney's dream had become a reality, but now we had a new challenge.

PART TWO

The Pioneering Years

1955–1960

EIGHTEEN

The Curtain's Up

During the formal dedication, Walt stuck to the script and recited the words which appear on the Disneyland plaque at the Town Square flagpole. But later, he came up with a quote which prophetic, and which we are still repeating:

Disneyland will never be completed as long as there is imagination in the world.

The fact was that we were *not* completed. One guest, after riding the trains, complained, "I had to pay 50 cents to see Walt Disney's backyard."

In terms of money, the park today is about 30 times what it was in 1955. In fact, just one attraction, Captain EO, which opened in 1986, cost $17 million, the same as the total cost of the park itself when we opened. Splash Mountain cost 5 times that original investment.

The curtain was up, the show was on the road, and now we had to learn how to operate this crazy dream. All theories and the plans were behind us. Now *we* were the ones selling the popcorn and keeping the gum off the seats.

We had real, live people to park, protect, feed, and entertain. And our rest rooms had to be clean. Walt willed it.

Since there had never been anything like Disneyland, there were no guidelines. These were truly Disneyland's pioneering days. We tried some crazy things and made some crazy mistakes. And yet it was a period during which many of our traditions were established. Just as Walt had checked every facet of construction, he now was everywhere, making his permanent imprint on his dream.

For me, the years, months, and days run together as the most exciting time of my life. I can't possibly put events in chronological order. Every day there was a new challenge, a new problem to be solved, perhaps a new mistake to be made.

If it hadn't been for Walt, the odds are that the doomsayers who predicted a spectacular failure would have been right. But Walt thrived on the challenges. He said, "I function better when things are going badly than when they're as smooth as whipped cream."

There was no whipped cream. If he had *designed* the challenges, they couldn't have been much tougher. As I remember them, they included:

Weather

Although we had received cooperation from nearly every source, the weather for that first year was the worst it could be. During the construction period, we had the wettest spring in 20 years—three weeks of rain. And then, just as we were getting started, it turned hot, hotter than the natives could remember, with 10 days of temperatures over 100 degrees. Attendance went to hell, and money dried up.

After the park opened, we always panicked when the rains came. If the weatherman said rain, we would call our people and tell them them to stay home, to save payroll costs. Then, the sun might come out and we'd be short of personnel.

Money

Walt referred to the money problem this way: "My biggest problem? Well, I'd say it's been my biggest problem all my life—MONEY. It takes a lot of money to make dreams come true. From the very start, it was a problem at Disneyland. I could never convince the financiers that Disneyland was feasible, because dreams offer too little collateral."

Every financial transaction was a cash transaction. One person was assigned to pick up the money at the main entrance and rush it to the bank before closing time. This was necessary to cover the checks which had to be written, such as the weekly payroll.

When salaried people and consultants were paid, they were sometimes asked to hold their paychecks for a few days until the money would come in to cover them.

Some suppliers, knowing our precarious financial situation, put us on a C.O.D. basis. That's "cash on delivery": no cash, no delivery.

In the rush toward opening day, many things had been done without any paper work or written approval. I had contributed about $20,000 for that Harbor off-ramp and food for my traffic control unit. In some way, the press found out that there was $900,000 of costs incurred without any records. When they asked Walt about it, he was not dismayed and said almost happily, "Well, if you do *big things*, you make *big mistakes*." *That* was real class.

Our White Wing, Trinidad

During the days of horse-drawn vehicles in Chicago, the clean-up men were called "White Wings". Walt not only insisted on having a White Wing for his Main Street, but he personally cast Trinidad for the job. At Walt's demand, Trinidad received extra pay, and for good reason.

For several years Trinidad was the most photographed person in the park, and on his days off he would come to the park just to make sure his replacement was doing the job.

Today, members of our Custodial staff still follow the horses, but in standard dress. After all, people today have never heard of a White Wing.

"NOT A REST ROOM?"

To avoid complaints about the long lines and broken-down attractions, we recruited some talented people from the studio to be attractions of another sort.

Roy Williams, the Big Moosketeer, drew Mickey for people on Main Street. One woman stood in line a long time for a Mickey picture and then exclaimed, "But, I thought this was a line for the rest room!"

So Much Else

On the day after opening, a gas leak was discovered in Fantasyland. We had to call in the Anaheim Fire Department and evacuate all the guests. It was a bit of excitement we didn't need.

Our "harvest season" was in August, when we could expect the most guests. We would schedule people for the busy weekend days, which seemed smart at the time. Unfortunately, people had heard about long lines and traffic jams on the weekends, and they stayed away. But then, on Mondays, when we didn't expect anyone, we would be jammed by all the people hoping to avoid the crowds.

Labor Day, based on our predictions, was supposed to be a *big* day for us. We had a dollar pool with estimates for that day's attendance. I hate to confess this, but I took the lowest number, something like 10,000 people, and I won. The word was out to avoid the crowds, and people stayed away in droves.

••

Walt's "Educated" Weeds

Ten years later, at the anniversary party for the pioneers, Walt recalled some of the difficulties we experienced in getting Disneyland opened.

"A lot of people don't realize that we had some serious problems keeping this thing going and getting it started. I remember when we opened, if anyone recalls, we didn't have enough money to finish the landscaping. And I had Bill Evans go out and put Latin tags on all the weeds."

••

Despite these problems, the first August brought in enough to give us encouragement. The money would come rolling in. But southern California kids do have to go back to school at the end of the summer. As a result, the week after Labor Day, Disneyland looked completely dead. When the first reports arrived at the studio, there was panic. Then, although our staff was already lean, we had to cut to the bone. The rumors flew, and insecurity was epidemic.

Walt didn't panic, but many of our lessees did, and blamed the low winter attendance on the "high" admission price of 95 cents. Finally, Walt squelched their attempts to lower the price by raising his right eyebrow and saying, "Don't tamper with my gate!"

During those first years, there was no Cal State Fullerton or University of California at Irvine to provide a source of personnel. Fortunately, the El Toro Marine Base was close at hand, and the Marines were available when we needed them. Since they weren't busy in the halls of Montezuma or the shores of Tripoli, they helped us out by operating the Disneyland dream.

One key to survival during these tough times was the weekly *Disneyland* TV show. It was not only what some called an "hour-long commercial for Disneyland", but was always great entertainment.

At one time, when the Jungle Cruise alligators weren't working, Walt commented, "I know damn well these work. I've seen it on television."

I was typical of others who watched the show religiously. It was reassuring to us to see the show as the guests saw it, in spite of our backstage concerns.

In my pre-Disneyland career, I'd been involved in creating several new organizations. As a result, I was interested in seeing how Walt used his genius in creating the team that created Disneyland.

Here I'd like to pause for a moment and explain my personal observation of how the Disneyland organization was put together...for it was unique in all of the entertainment industry, and in the entire business world, for that matter.

One of my favorite Walt TV interviews is the one with Fletcher Markle of the Canadian Broadcasting Corporation. Although I never saw it on American TV, I've enjoyed the tape many times and have used it in our training programs.

When asked about his most important accomplishment, Walt answered, "To build this organization...and to *keep it together.*"

Early on, Walt had dictated that we weren't going to hire any people with amusement park experience. When it was suggested, he answered that: "First, Disneyland is *not* an amusement park. Second, we're going to hire some young people who are willing to learn. We'll make mistakes, but we'll learn from them."

Walt had done his own careful research of old-time amusement parks and fairs, and the policy was we would not hire anyone who had such experience.

This policy ended up creating an organization which contained a rainbow of diverse talents and experience at Disneyland.

The Brothers Team

In Walt's generation, there were many famous brother teams. In autos, the Dodge Brothers; in movies, the Warner Brothers.

Walt Disney and his older brother Roy were at the heart of the Disney organization. The legend was, Walt was the creative genius and Roy the financial genius. It was (and still is) my observation that Walt was a very practical businessman, and that Roy understood the show. After Walt's death, Roy moved right in to the forefront of the business, combining the two talents.

Both brothers had grown up through the so-called "school of hard knocks". They knew as much about construction and financing as they did about filmed entertainment.

It was a totally unique team, and there would be no Disneyland had it not been for their *combination* of talents and experience.

The Entrenched, Talented, Studio Personnel

These were the brilliant people who had been around long enough to know Walt, his methods, his likes, his dislikes. They were producing the movies and TV shows which made Disneyland possible.

I've mentioned that Walt said, "We have no geniuses at the studio." To me, people like Ken Anderson and Herb Ryman *were* geniuses—but they were unassuming, friendly, and loyal.

The WED Imagineers

To avoid the negative thinking from some at the studio and among the stockholders, Walt created a separate group comprised of true believers in his dream. At first, he paid them from his personal funds and eventually included them on the studio payroll.

When he received criticism, he separated a group of creative artists, architects, and engineers from the rest of his staff.

Together, they formed a group called WED, an acronym for Walter Elias Disney. This was to be the elite group for creating Disneyland and all future outdoor projects. (Now it's called Walt Disney Imagineering.)

Woody's Team

Within this group of creative entertainment talents, Wood formed his own team of people who were selected on the basis of their proven abilities… and loyalty. They included people from Stanford Research, associates from aircraft and industry, some very competent Texans, and me.

Wood was an organizational genius in his own right, and he was probably the only man who could work between Walt and Roy while making his own imprint on the future organization.

Those of us on Wood's team were accustomed to plans, policies, and procedures. We liked job descriptions and neat organizational charts where every person had his or her little box.

This line of thinking was alien to the way the creative studio people worked. Walt explained it very well: "You get in…we call them gag sessions. We get in there and toss ideas around. And we throw them in and put all the minds together and come up with something, then we say a little prayer and open it and hope it will go."

As a result, when we came up with charts and procedures, the creative studio people called it "AIRCRAFT thinking". And they properly told us we had to learn "SHOW thinking".

The Institutional Lessees

Perhaps Disneyland might not have been able to weather the financial crisis if it hadn't been for a bit of Woody's brilliance.

He sold Walt, who didn't normally like "outsiders", on bringing in institutional lessees, such as Swift and Company, Eastman Kodak, and Upjohn Pharmacy. And then he sold *them* on the value of being involved in this Disney dream. They paid for their exhibits…and their staffs.

The Contract Lessees

That original four million estimated cost was ballooning every day. We made contracts for most of the needed services for which we couldn't pay. These included parking, food, merchandise, crowd control, custodial maintenance, sound and skilled maintenance, and security.

In addition, there was a group of consultants, including me, whose contracts were week-to-week, and usually on a handshake basis.

All live entertainment was contracted. The Disneyland Band and the Golden Horseshoe Revue had longer contracts—two weeks in length.

As anyone who watched a Western movie knows, the West was won by a strange mix of adventurers, drunks, gunslingers, church people, bankers, and cattlemen fighting farmers and their fences.

There was a frontier spirit at Disneyland, and we had our share of characters. Some were just looking for a job. Others were looking for a fast buck, and still others were attracted by the magic of Walt Disney's name. A few were even crooked (or "creatively dishonest", if you prefer):

- There was a parking lot foreman who regularly came back from Las Vegas with several thousands of dollars in winnings. It turned out that the money was *really* won by reselling parking lot tickets.

- There was the bachelor who claimed ten children as deductions on his income tax form. The IRS picked him up at the Golden Horseshoe where he worked. The guests thought it was part of the show.

- There was a merchandise promoter who had to borrow money from Fred Schumacher when he first landed in Santa Ana. After only six months, he owned an expensive, prestigious home. Kickbacks from lessees paid for it.

- And there was the charming guy who always had hamburgers when I needed them. He stole credit cards, a unique enterprise in those days, and then charged fur coats on them. He also was led from the Magic Kingdom in handcuffs.

Three decades later, we tend to hire people who fit the "Disney Image"— healthy and clean-cut. But in those pioneering days, Central Casting could not have selected a more diverse group of people.

Things could be tough, but Walt had a way of reaching out and boosting a person's morale and jump-starting one's dedication.

One day, walking past the Hills Brothers coffee shop on Main Street, Walt hailed me from over his table where he was sitting with his brother-in-law, Bill Cottrell. He asked me to sit down, and then he said, "I've been meaning to tell you, Van, you're doing a great job on the training program."

I forget what else was said over the coffee.

But that was a shot in the arm which would keep me going to months, maybe years.

Despite the good times we all shared, none of us—including me—thought of Disneyland as a career job. And with money so tight, there was no sense of security.

At the time of Disneyland's 25th anniversary, however, 84 of the pioneers of 1955 were still around and working. The group diminishes, but after 35 years, about four dozen of us still get together to reminisce. Some have moved on to key jobs in just about every entertainment enterprise in the country.

During that first year, I was too busy and having too much fun to worry about my future, even though I was still on a week-to-week handshake deal. Dick had been picked by Fred Schumacher to head up the Mail Room, and I had to take over his training duties. I'd also become an "expert" in community relations, and I'd give talks to service clubs. I was trying to follow Walt's example by getting out in the park, talking to people, and finding out about show business.

I love confusion. I was working seven days a week, but happy. Some things are too good to last.

NINETEEN

Off to Tomorrowland

The White House continued as a coffee shop for the Highway Patrol and as my base of operations. I'd acquired another temporary resident: Bill Hansen of the Wonderland Music Company was setting up shop for Disney records and other music labels on Main Street. He needed an office, and Jack Olsen sent him to see me. We made a perfect combination—he had records, and I had Disneyland passes.

Bill was also good on the piano at the Gourmet Bar. On one occasion, he sang his own song, which went like this:

> *Everything is fine...in Anaheim.*
> *Things must be rustin' in Tustin, but*
> *Everything is fine...in Anaheim.*

I may have missed a phrase, but that's how I remember it. After his "Anaheim" song, he went into "I Want a Big, Fat Woman to Tell My Troubles To". People would ask him to play other tunes, but on that night, *all* he would play was the big, fat woman song.

At least, *I* liked it, and life was just perfect, until another call from Wood temporarily terminated any contemplation about what I was going to do with the rest of my life. I headed over to Wood's office, and he got right to the point: "Van, Jack Reilley is being transferred from Tomorrowland to head up the Engineering Department. Walt's been impressed by what you've done, and we think you can take over as manager of Tomorrowland."

Sitting next to Woody was Admiral Joe Fowler. Since he was one of Disneyland's most important pioneers, he deserves a special introduction before I get on with my own story.

While I was at the studio, Woody had introduced me to Joe Fowler. He made sure I knew that Joe was directly responsible to Walt for the construction at Disneyland. I had learned that it was a good idea to find out everything I could about people I might meet or work with. In this case, I checked *Who's Who in America*. Sure enough, Joe's career was covered in great detail.

During those pre-opening days, I had a special name for Admiral Joseph Fowler: "Can Do, the Magician". Walt would ask him to do some impossible task, and his answer would be a positive "CAN DO!" He could raise hell when required, but if he agreed to some request, even one of mine, the conversation would end with "CAN DO!"

Walt gave him a testimonial at our tenth anniversary party which was more fun than the *Who's Who* write-up:

> Oh, I can go back to Joe Fowler. We went up there...we had to have somebody who could really put this thing together, somebody who could take hold of this thing and really make it work. So we were told about this retired admiral.
>
> He had run the San Francisco Navy Yard, had built ships in China, and all that. And he was starting a sub-division in San Jose. So I remember, we went to see him. We met Joe at his home with his lovely wife, and we had dinner together.
>
> And we had steaks that were wonderful, so we sort of prevailed upon him to come down and be a consultant for us. And, little by little, we got him trapped into this thing. We got him so trapped that he said, "To hell with the subdivision!"

For Disneyland and Disney World, that dinner in San Jose was critical. Walt and Joe made an unbeatable team...building Disneyland's own navy.

I was recently in Florida, and Dick Nunis took me to Joe's 95th birthday party. Although still active with developments in Florida, Joe had also built a farm on his birthplace in Maine, and was proud of building "the largest barn in the State of Maine".

I asked him if he'd be flying out to our next reunion on our Disneyland birthday and his answer was, you guessed it, "CAN DO!"

But back on that day in 1955, Joe was to become my new boss, and I was to become the manager of Tomorrowland for one of the longest months and most frustrating periods in my whole damn Disneyland career.

I warned both Wood and Joe that I was qualified as a training specialist, but—and I'd proven it to myself—a lousy administrator. They still wanted me to take the job. On the other hand, I had found out that if you were offered a different job in a corporation, you'd better take it. There was no choice.

So I asked, "When do you want me to start?" Since it was Saturday, I figured my starting day would be that Monday...which it was.

Of all the lands at Disneyland, at the time of opening, Tomorrowland suffered the most from shortages of time, talent, and money. It was hot and barren. Electrical systems broke down all the time. The Phantom Boats were constantly stopping in mid-stream.

The operators called Autopia "Blood Alley", with some justification. The cars did not run on rails then, and there were no safety belts or protection from the steering wheels. As a result, giving first aid to the young drivers who had their teeth knocked out was a frequent activity.

Although it is not mentioned in the history books, right there in Tomorrowland a rocket ship went to the moon and back *before* the Russians launched their Sputnik in 1956. To launch *our* rocket ship, we had a pneumatic system which, when it was operating properly, would shake the passengers at take-off and landing. Unfortunately, this system would break down all too often, and the guests would receive a very quiet ride.

In Tomorrowland, as well as other areas of the park, some of the best attractions were the live ones. At the time, our spaceman was a young man named John Catone who would later become a prominent manager at Disneyland. During the World Series, John would carry a radio inside his space suit so he could give us timely updates on the score. Our female space cadets were also a big attraction.

Tomorrowland was a potential place for youthful gangs to congregate, and I was not only the wrong size to handle such situations, but I was also a coward. Fortunately, our security and the Anaheim police prevented any major problems.

It didn't take a month for me—and for Wood and Joe—to understand that this was not my area of expertise. After 30 days and 30 nights of what was sort of a nightmare, I caught the flu, and was absent for *one* day. Back then, if you missed one day, people would ask, "Where have you been?"

When I returned after that one day, Wood and Joe invited me back for another meeting in the same office. I had been tipped off that I would be replaced, and I hoped that Wood and Joe would feel slightly guilty about making a mistake, since I had warned them. I tried to make it easier for them by remarking, "I know you didn't call me in to ask about my cold."

"Van," Wood began, "we have a real need for a training program for our foremen. Your program in Texas worked well, and we need something like that." He added, "How long will it take to clear out your office?" I affirmed that one day would be more than enough.

People and jobs changed rapidly in those days, and my replacement, Howard Vineyard, didn't know whether I had been told of my departure. Nor did he know that I felt like I was getting out of jail. My secretary in the Tomorrowland office was the widow of one of Joe Fowler's Navy friends, and she lived by the rulebook. The *rule* was that a new host or hostess didn't report to my office without being in costume. My Navy-trained secretary wouldn't let Howard in, since he wasn't "properly" dressed. He finally had to tell her that he was her new boss.

Howie was one of Wood's younger Texans. He had left an advertising job in Denver to join Disneyland. Although he was brash, he was sensitive, and he thought I would be heartbroken at being moved out of Tomorrowland. When I welcomed him with open arms we were both relieved, and at the end of the day we met at the Gourmet Bar at the Disneyland Hotel to celebrate.

Two positive things came out of my 30-day nightmare in Tomorrowland:

- I developed a life-long appreciation for the managers who oversee operations of the various lands. These individuals have to be skilled in a broad range of functions. Perhaps it may be a bit easier now than it was for me in the first year, but the managers must still be qualified in *everything* that goes on, from human relations to safety to engineering to guest relations.

- I developed a life-long relationship with Jack Reilley, whom I had replaced as manager of Tomorrowland. Jack had been a Navy engineering officer who had worked with Joe Fowler. Years later, at a meeting of the 1955 pioneers, Jack came up with a name for us: PAMOTL, or PAST AREA MANAGER OF TOMORROW LAND.

Like me, Jack had been miscast as an area manager. Before Tomorrowland, he had been a key person in the building of the park. Now he would return to be chief engineer, a position in which his talents were profitably put to use at Disneyland and later at Walt Disney World.

Fortunately, I could retreat to the White House to begin a new career doing interesting things for which I was qualified. Joe Fowler brought together those of us who were or had been managers, and for the first and last time, I received a $50 bill as a bonus.

At the end of the summer, some of us who had been working on a week-to-week basis were officially brought on the payroll, which brought a regular paycheck, benefits, even vacations.

I signed up immediately. I bought a house. I was too busy to contemplate my future. I didn't even think of quitting.

Autopia

Doc Lemmon had an idea of painting all the Autopia cars grey, a neutral color which was easier to maintain and more economical.

Walt blasted that idea by saying, "Dammit, this is a show! These cars are part of the show!"

And that was that.

TWENTY

Back to the White House

Fortunately, the White House was still there, and I was happy to get back to my orange groves and coffee with Mrs. Mohn.

I was handling leader orientation and traffic and highway programs, but Wood was right in feeling that we had to train people in leadership and show business.

This was but one of the programs which have been expanded over the years, and was the first produced from that old White House on West Street

It was great for my ego to leave a job for which I was not qualified and get back to creating training programs, a task that suited me well from my days as an education manager in Texas.

I needed help, and at the time, there was no way I could hire an assistant. So I *borrowed* people. Milo Rainey was a foreman on the Jungle Cruise, and on his own time he had designed the best training program for his guides that I had ever seen. So Milo helped me with my new program, which I called "Foreman/Lead Development". If you want to know the difference between a "foreman" and a "lead", there really wasn't any.

Regardless of title, these are people who are union members and are paid by the hour, but they're also the ones who train other cast members.

The program taught purely the basics: training, methods, human relations, communications. Today, it would have the fancy name of "Management Development".

One problem we dealt with was a common one in new organizations. People would bitch and moan about everything, not taking action, just blaming others.

I decided to try an unusual technique for dealing with this situation. I asked Milo to get a box of dry horse droppings from the Pony Farm. I set the droppings on the conference table with this question: "Are you just going to complain about it, or shall we find a way to clean up the problem?"

It wouldn't work today, but it did then.

I can say with some pride that nearly all of the men, and there were only men in those days, in that first group went on to become supervisors. That's not a bad batting average.

Then, once again, Woody had an idea. "What we need around here is a recreation club, something that will help people to have fun off the job."

By this time I had learned from Joe Fowler to say, "CAN DO!" I had had some experience, but I needed help...a lot of help. So I formed a committee.

I selected the committee members to reflect the diversity of our cast. Once again, I asked for help from Dick Nunis and Milt Albright, along with others. Wood said we could have the profits from the snack vending machines in the park break areas. Big deal! A few hundred bucks.

Milt Albright had a better idea. At the time, we still had some pay toilets in the park. Guests had the mistaken idea that for 10 cents the seats were cleaner. Milt suggested that we get those receipts—about $700 a month. We tried, but Larry Tryon, the finance director, caught us in the act. We were told that it was too much money *just* for recreation.

At any rate we *had* a club, with bowling leagues, parties, and even classes in art and design. The Disneyland Recreation Club (today called Cast Activities) is now one of the best in the country, with a budget and a staff. But I can recall its humble beginnings.

In addition to our White House on West Street, another old home on the site had escaped destruction—the Brown House. We took over that home and made it our club headquarters. But we needed someone to coordinate the club's functions, and we had no money to pay such a person.

Chuck Whelan introduced me to a charming woman with a charming name—Donna Rochelle. I explained our situation to her, but Donna wasn't worried about not getting paid. She said she would take over the job and then speculate on how to get paid. We made a deal. And how *did* we pay her? We would sell merchandise, saying: "Support your recreation club!" We started a newspaper and sold ad space. One of our best supporters was Jan Ayers, who was in charge of Group Insurance. Her husband had a Chevrolet agency in Laguna Beach, and he would advertise in our little newspaper.

With the snack machine receipts and the fund raisers, we managed to pay Donna enough to get the club going. Perhaps our greatest asset was Donna's charm. She could charm people into doing things which they wouldn't do for me.

Life in the Brown House was primitive, even for those times. At one committee meeting, the members asked me what Donna did. This is a "short" version of her days: "Well, in the morning she starts some coffee, then sweeps up the place. Since there is no heat, in cold weather she starts a fire in the fireplace." The members thought I was kidding, but I wasn't.

In one way or another, the club grew, and we finally got Donna on the payroll. Eventually, she got a job with the lessee who operated the Mexican Village, and then was hired by the Insurance Company of America, where she supervised their Disneyland activities for 18 years.

One day the club would require a staff and a budget, but with enthusiastic volunteers, we did a lot of things. Here was something for nearly everyone: an active bowling league, an annual employee Christmas party, an art club, money-raising dances.

It was a lot of fun and—in those early days of short money—the more activities I had, the more job security I felt.

TWENTY-ONE

The Walt Disney School of Trial-and-Error Management

Long before Disneyland's opening, Walt had rejected the idea of hiring a professional "amusement park" team. He realized that we'd make mistakes, but knew we'd learn from them.

I had the perfect spot. I never worked directly for Walt, but for people who did. I understand that if he was mad, he'd raise a very expressive eyebrow as a warning. And, I'm told, if he was bored at some presentation, he might tap his ring on the table. I never encountered those mannerisms, but I don't remember anyone getting fired for coming up with a dumb idea of making a mistake.

There was no curriculum, but the Walt Disney School of Trial-and-Error Management was in session every day, with Walt as the head instructor.

What follows is a kaleidoscope summary of my memories of the events that ended up with the creation of an entirely new breed of theme park management.

"You Lose Money on Peak Days"

George Whitney was the only consultant from an amusement park whom Walt had hired. He was brilliant, and the owner of "Whitney's at the Beach" in San Francisco.

One day, when the park was busy, George and I were having lunch, and I made some comment about the crowds. "Never forget, Van," he told me, "that you *lose* money on the peak days."

I didn't understand him, and he had to patiently explain this maxim of our business. "People come to Disneyland to *spend* money, not to save it. If they are standing in long lines, they can't spend their money."

He figures that in the early days we lost about $1.00 for every hour a person stood in a line.

The Day After Christmas

During the weeks before Christmas, people stayed away in droves. As a result, we weren't ready for the MOBS which came as soon as people had opened their presents and wanted to come to Disneyland.

The Best Audience...Walt

Walt would always take guests to the Golden Horseshoe Revue. Over the years, he probably saw the show several hundred times. Wally Boag commented that "Walt was our best audience. He'd always laugh at the right time, and participate as if it were the first time he'd seen the show."

It was a good lesson for me, and I passed it on to my children. If one is going to see a live show, one has an obligation to applaud the performers.

Dunked in a Story Book

Ken Anderson was art director for Storybook Land, and he gave me tours of this new 1956 attraction while it was being built. Finally, it was ready for opening, and he took me along on a row boat for final inspection. I was thrilled. I was also wearing a suit.

When he dropped me off at the dock, I forgot that it was curved. As I said "that was great!" I walked right into five feet of water. It was embarrassing to slosh my way down Main Street to Wardrobe, where I could borrow some clothes.

"I Want That Train Running!"

Doc Lemmon had to learn about Walt's concern for guests the hard way. The problem then was, as it is now, to keep costs down by not scheduling too many people.

It was Saturday, and Walt was late for a meeting with his key people. He came in wearing what was called his "wounded bear look"...dangerous. He had noticed a long line of guests waiting for the Disneyland Railroad train. Doc and his staff had scheduled only one of our two trains. "Why," Walt asked, "is the second train not operating?"

Doc explained that he hadn't anticipated the attendance and was saving money by using only the one train. This was perhaps exactly the wrong thing to say. As the story was told to me, Walt glared and forcibly made a point which was rough and educational.

"As the president, chairman of the board, and general head man around here, *I want that other train running...and NOW!"*

For the first time, Doc and his supervisors rushed out and personally operated the second train. Later, when Walt saw Doc looking down and harried, he put his arm around him and said, "Doc, never lose your sense of humor!"

The Hippos Didn't Always Hop

The Jungle Cruise concept has been copied many times. But in 1955, it was an innovation. Walt had moved from animation to live-action movies, and *this* was a LIVE, live-action show.

The Jungle Cruise instantly became the most popular attraction in Disneyland. Walt spent more time checking it out than he spent on some of his films. We would be warned that he and Lilly were heading to his apartment located above the Fire Station on Main Street. And then, his first inspection stop was the Jungle Cruise.

On one occasion, having been warned of Walt's impending arrival, everyone was told to make sure that the experimental animation was working. Unfortunately, it was complicated, and sometimes it would break down, usually just as Walt arrived.

There were two unsung heroes in the Maintenance division who found that the crocodiles were not snapping just as Walt reached the scene. They hid in the foliage and worked the animation by hand.

A Very Special Cruise

By 1956, Disneyland had become a key stop on the State Department's V.I.P. list. One visiting dignitary was President Sukarno of Indonesia, who will never be forgotten.

He and his entourage visited the park in the afternoon and then left for a scheduled tour of a shopping center. Just as the park was closing, we received an emergency message: "The president wants to come back to take the Jungle Cruise again."

We closed the park and then reopened the Jungle Cruise for Sukarno. He was a great audience, backing away from the snakes and ducking under Schweitzer Falls. He loved it!

Dick Is Tripped Up on Trip Time

Dick Nunis had started out his career with some very interesting assignments, serving a lot of key people—including me.

He had proved to be exceptionally competent and dedicated; a fantastic worker. Fred Schumacher had been impressed and had the clout to steal Dick for his division. Unfortunately, he was supervisor of the Mail Room!

Over the years, Dick has been in many tough situations, but I've never seen him so low as when he was sitting behind a desk in the Mail Room!

Without question, it is a good training experience. One learns about all the people in every nook and cranny of the park. But Dick hated it. Fortunately, Doc Lemmon rescued him, and he began a new career as manager of Adventureland and Frontierland.

Dick charged into the new assignment as he charges into everything, but he soon received a classic lesson from the chief mentor, Walt Disney.

A "trip time" of seven minutes had been established for the Jungle Cruise ride. That is the length of the trip from when the guests waves to other guests at departure to the "mother-in-law" joke at the conclusion. When there were hundreds of people lined up on a hot day, the operators tended to speed up the trip, and Walt was a passenger on one of these abbreviated trips.

Dick was standing on the dock when Walt steamed up with his eyebrows raised. "Dick, what is the trip time for this attraction?"

"Well, sir, it is seven minutes," Dick responded. Mad as hell, Walt came back with, "Well, I just had a *four-minute ride* and went through the hippo pool so fast I couldn't tell if they were rhinos or hippos." After being completely chewed out by Walt, Dick made a very bright career decision. He asked Walt if he had time to ride with him and explain *how* he wanted the ride to work.

Walt took the time. He spent an hour explaining how the sequences should work and how to play the show, because it is show business. "If the trip time is seven minutes, and you cut out three minutes, it's like going to a movie and having some important reels left out."

Dick instituted a concentrated training program. A week later, Walt came back for a review. Dick recalled, "Walt felt I might have stacked the deck with the best operator, so he went around with five different hosts. When he finally left after his last trip, Walt gave me a smile and a "thumbs-up" sign. I'd learned a valuable lesson."

The Queen in the Jungle

Tom Meslovich was skipper of the Jungle Cruise boat just in front of the one carrying the queen of Sweden and a group of Secret Service agents. His engine began to stall.

The queen and the Secret Service agents had been told of the two customary pistol shots in the Hippo Pool. But the emergency signal for a stalled boat engine was three shots, and six for a derail.

Tom imagined, correctly, that three shots might send the Secret Service into panic. He nursed the sputtering boat through the hippos and the natives with spears, until he could get near enough to the dock to be towed in. He was honored for his valiant efforts with an award presented at the end of the summer at the infamous Banana Ball.

Birth of Ticket Books

Ed Ettinger and I were having a drink when he told me about his idea.

At that time a rumor was making the rounds that it cost $0 to visit Disneyland. This was nearly impossible, unless the guest bought out the Pendleton shop and several other stores.

"Well, Van," Ed said, "I'll be a hero or a goat, but we're coming up with something called a ticket book to counter this prime resistance."

Fortunately, the idea worked...

You'll remember that I'd first been told admission to Disneyland would be 25 cents for adults and 15 cents for children..."just to keep the undesirables out". (Don't laugh about those prices. After all, a cup of coffee was only 5 cents.) Some Anaheim residents told me they were first told there would be no admission price for Disneyland. It would be a *free* park.

Walt had come up with the preview price of 95 cents for general admission. Then there were prices for each attraction. Walt had squelched any attempts to lower that price, saying "Don't tamper with my gate" with an eyebrow raised.

The ticket book was a way of tampering with the gate which didn't *seem* to be tampering with it. And it countered the $40 rumor. With lettered coupons, we could advertise admission to Disneyland and eight rides of your choice for $2.50. It was an answer to the rumors and proved to be effective in many other ways.

Young people learned about financial planning by the use of the "E" ticket—the prime ticket for the top attractions. It also served to encourage people to try rides that appeared less exciting, since they'd already paid for tickets for those rides, as part of the ticket book, and couldn't use them for anything else.

Over the years, that original ticket book was altered in many ways. It ended up that there were about 18 ways to visit Disneyland—with the Big 15 book at the top of the list.

An "E" ticket became part of American culture, symbolizing the *best*.

(One reason I miss the ticket books is that, thanks to my work with city, county, and state officials, I was always able to get complimentary passes and ticket books, even when they were well-controlled. In some cases, the cause was legitimate. On the other hand, I must confess, they were also helpful in getting free meals, drink, and other special services.)

Bob Hope Gets Some Lines

Charlie Jimenez is now a vice president of a major hotel and resort corporation. He travels around the world, hearing and living exciting stories in his work. But he remembers being a Jungle Cruise skipper and the day that Bob Hope rode in his boat.

Bob was a great audience, and he laughed at all of the jokes and anecdotes Charlie told during the trip. At the end of the ride, Bob started the applause for Charlie and then thanked him for the lines.

And Charlie remembers that he graciously told Bob Hope that he could use any of those lines...free of charge.

"Tommy the Toe"

Tommy Walker was probably responsible for more show ideas than anyone else in the organization. And fortunately for him, he was protected by Walt's trial-and-error approach to learning.

Walt had met Tommy when Walt's daughter Diane and his future son-in-law, Ron Miller, attended USC.

Tommy had achieved some local celebrity as "Tommy the Toe". At football games he would lead the USC Band, and he was the best I've ever seen. Then, when the game began, he would put on a football uniform to perform his specialty, kicking the point after touchdown.

Tommy was a pain in the ass for many of our executives, since he would go directly to Walt to sell his ideas.

He left Disneyland after about ten years and went on to achieve fame for producing spectacular shows such as the opening and closing ceremonies for the Summer Olympics of 1984 and the dedication of the Statute of Liberty in 1986.

Many of Tommy's ideas worked well and have become part of our Disneyland tradition. They include our Christmas parade, the fireworks show, the balloon ascensions for our special events, the Disneyland tour guides, and our Christmas candlelight show.

Orchids on Main Street

One of our most wonderful, spectacular "learning experiences" was our first great Easter program.

As it was planned, the choir would be singing on the steps of the Main Street Railroad Station. At the finale of the program, a helicopter was to come down over Town Square. An Easter Bunny in the helicopter would throw out orchids which were to drift down on the watching audience.

There were two unanticipated problems:

As the helicopter descended on Town Square, the propellers sucked up everything that wasn't tied down—skirts, sheet music, hats, branches, and other stray objects.

The orchids were frozen, like frozen lima beans (but much larger). Since the Easter Bunny's contract instructed him to throw the flowers, he did just that, dumping the frozen orchids, which dropped with thuds when they struck the asphalt around the confused and then terrified guests.

Storybook Glass

An art director was showing Walt a model of one of the little houses in Pinocchio's Village, part of the Storybook Land Canal Boats ride.

He justified using cheaper glass by saying, "The guests can't see it." That remark drew a raised eyebrow from Walt and the comment, "*I* can see it."

And that was that!

Frontierland Shootouts

Our regular gunfight shows were fun for guests who might otherwise be standing in a line. We could get double duty out of two men assigned to Security.

Black Bart had no trouble playing an old-time robber, since he was sort of a sleazy type by nature. Sergeant Lucky was an easy-going, friendly man who could play the good sheriff when he and Black Bart had their regular shootouts in front of the Golden Horseshoe.

Unfortunately, they wanted the rates of Hollywood stunt men, and their shows finally bit the dust during one of our frequent budget cuts.

The Mouseketeers

The Mouseketeers were at the peak of their TV popularity and were regularly brought to Disneyland to entertain our guests. Young people *do* grow up, but many of that group have remained in show business.

Now, more than 35 years later, many of the original group appear in special live shows and parades.

Mermaids and Submarines

The Submarine Adventure was our first major attraction to be added after opening. I didn't believe it would be successful, thinking that everyone (like myself) had claustrophobia. I was wrong, of course.

To add to the new attraction's show, Tommy Walker came up with the idea of using real live mermaids. I watched the auditions at the Disneyland Hotel...definitely a fringe benefit. The mermaids provided a good show, but it was almost too good, since our scuba diving maintenance men would often take extra trips out to make sure they were all right.

Our Circus Came to Town

Walt had been warned by Walter Knott about the weeks before Christmas. Knott told him that the public seemed to forget at the same time each year that there was a Knott's Berry Farm.

Well, we didn't want the public to forget Disneyland, so Walt—or somebody—came up with an idea for changing that pattern of visitors. We'd call it the Mickey Mouse Club Circus.

For me, and for some others, it was a wonderful experience. People were needed for the character parade, and I could dress up and walk around in a parade in the almost Big Top.

I was working in the White House, which had become headquarters for the performers. I found out how people could get "sawdust in the veins". If I had been a kid, I might have joined the group.

There were all sorts of memorable circus events which *weren't* planned:

- On opening night, the female trapeze artist lost her brassiere while flying through the air with the greatest of ease.
- The llamas would not only spit, but would attempt to escape by running down Main Street with Doc Lemmon and his staff in pursuit.
- The lions in Professor Keller's famous lion act had been declawed and tranquilized. The Professor's greatest fear was that one of them would go to sleep and fall on him.

Although almost *any* circus is a good draw, this one was an expensive learning experience, losing around $375,000. We learned some other things:

- It was impossible to compete with Santa Claus and Christmas shopping. *No* show could have done it.
- We didn't need a special show the week *after* Christmas. We had more guests than we could handle without it.
- And then nothing could buck the public's "stay away" mood after New Year's.

Very quickly, the circus performers left my White House...and not too long after that, the art director who had been primarily responsible for the circus was looking for a job at another studio.

More than 30 years later another circus, Circus Fantasy, came to Disneyland. I had my doubts, but fortunately I kept my mouth shut. The new circus, produced during the show days of March, was a big success.

The Disneyland Band

The Disneyland Band, under the direction of Vesey Walker, Tommy's father, was originally hired for only two weeks. They became a tradition and have now marched enough miles to set a record for the longest continuous march in history.

The Fireworks

It wasn't easy getting the city's approval for our first Fantasy in the Sky fireworks display. They finally went along with it. The fireworks *do* make a lot of noise, and some neighbors complained. But the critics were out-numbered by the residents who enjoyed them. On the night of our first display, people "ooh'd" and "aah'd" as each rocket was launched.

And then behind me I heard a loud "WOW!" It was Walt having fun with his guests. Outside the park, the fireworks caused traffic problems. People would drive to the area and then park to watch the nightly displays. There had been fireworks before, and today they are commonplace in many spectaculars. But that first Fantasy in the Sky had been choreographed as a Disneyland show. If Walt said "WOW!", it had to be good.

We sure did make a lot of mistakes, but as Walt had told us, we'd "learn from our mistakes", and we *did* learn, while having a lot of fun, too.

TWENTY-TWO

Memories of Past Attractions

Perhaps our attractions were less expensive in the fifties and sixties, but we thought most of them were pretty good. Some left to cheers, others to tears.

Space Station X-1

This was a diorama by a great artist, Peter Ellenshaw. It was a walk-through which gave you a view of the earth from outer space.

The Mickey Mouse Theatre

Our Disney cartoons were shown in this theatre in Fantasyland. It was also used for our cast meetings and pep talks, which were sometimes called "A Brainwash in the Mouse House".

The Phantom Boats

It was the era of those big tail fins on large cars, and these boats had huge tail fins, too. An attraction for children, replaced by the Motor Boat Cruise.

20,000 Leagues Under the Sea

One Tomorrowland attraction was a replica of the submarine in the award-winning film, *20,000 Leagues Under the Sea*. It had been created, from start to finish, in two weeks, with Walt helping out by painting the giant squid.

The Rainbow Cavern Mine Ride

This was one of my favorites, and it entertained millions before it was replaced by Big Thunder. When Walt first rode the train, he was unhappy with the spiel, and I was elected to revise it.

The View Liner

Walt loved his trains, and this was an early version of the monorail. When it was replaced, it ended up in Marceline, Missouri, at Disney Park.

The Conestoga Wagons

Another attraction that was short-lived was the ride on our Conestoga wagons. We stopped this immediately when one of the horses tripped, tipping the wagon over...fortunately with only minor guest injuries.

The Dairy Place

The American Dairy Association, one of our early institutional lessees, sponsored the Dairy Bar exhibit in Tomorrowland. The lessee paid for the design and construction, and for the people who staffed the exhibit. Walt called it "found money"...and we certainly needed it.

The Indian Village

The Indian Village was located where Bear Country is now. Guests were entertained with authentic dances from such tribes as the Apache, Navajo, Comanche, and Pawnee. But the show biz experience created problems with some of the performers. They felt that their next stop was the movies and demanded higher wages. We also found out that the Indians we hired to paddle our war canoes had never seen canoes or paddles before, and needed special training. One advantage of mechanical animation is that machines don't demand higher wages and longer coffee breaks.

Mule Pack

The mules in our Mule Pack ride didn't object to their pay, but their feeding and care became a burden, and they were eventually replaced by a Frontierland expansion and the Big Thunder Mountain Railroad.

Portrait Artists

I had a special feeling for the portrait artists who worked in the little street by the Market House. They were Jack Olsen's idea. Not only did they add to the Main Street show, but they also provided extra revenue to the company and, as a bonus, a good living for the artists. All the artists had good training, but the problem was to teach them to do a portrait in no more than seven minutes. It was a good show for Disneyland a good venture for the artists. Unfortunately, they thought we could not live without them. They were replaced with an artificial flower market. I hated to see them go.

Holidayland

Milt Albright came up with the idea of a special area at the park with a separate entrance to be made available for special parties for companies and organizations. The place would be called Holidayland. There would be a tent for meetings, ball fields, and play areas. Although Disneyland was totally dry, here there would be beer. Unfortunately, it was almost impossible to get enough temporary rest rooms to handle the beer consumption. In addition, some of the guests would get sloshed on beer and come into the park that way. Holidayland died a natural death within a year, but Milt had proven his promotional abilities and moved ahead to the successful development of the Magic Kingdom Club.

Monsanto House of the Future

On the edge of Tomorrowland stood the Monsanto House of the Future, a perfect addition to the theme in 1957. It was a proud monument to the plastic optimism of the Eisenhower years. It was on my "must-see" list when I brought visitors to the park. But then came the movement toward "natural" and the fashion-conscious began to sneer at the Melmac and Naugahyde. The House of the Future was replaced with lovely, natural landscaping, but not without a fight. We knocked down many structures as Disneyland grew and changed, and the Monsanto House was the toughest to tear down...a tribute to the endurance of plastics.

Aunt Jemima

Disneyland has always been a reflection of America, and some changes resulted from new attitudes in our society. Aunt Jemima had fit right in on the banks of the Rivers of America in 1955. But during the turbulent 60s, the Civil Rights movement fought against such black stereotypes. We kept the pancakes, but the popular breakfast place became the River Belle Terrace.

Flying Saucers

One of our most innovative, and one of my favorite, attractions was the Flying Saucers. Here you would climb into little round boats and be pushed up by forced air, moving around as you guided your little saucer. I considered them my occupational therapy. When things got tough, I'd go out and fly. Unfortunately, the concept was a bit ahead of the technology, and a financial loser.

There were continuing changes in attractions and facilities. And now I had to cope with the first major change to affect the people in the organization.

TWENTY-THREE

End of the Wood Era

Things were going well for me—if not as smooth as whipped cream, at least they were interesting, and as insecure as I am, I wasn't worrying.

I think there is a difference between a network and a grapevine. My network included people with whom I worked and who supported me... sort of a mutual assistance relationship. But the grapevine is something else. It deals with gossip and rumors and has no beginning or end. You might pick up a tip from anybody, even someone who doesn't work for the organization.

And the squeezings from the grapevine were most disturbing. The rumor was that Walt and Wood were not getting along, and that Wood's job was in danger.

Soon the rumor became face. In 1954, Wood said, "Walt treats me like a son," and now he was out. In retrospect, the break-up seems like an inevitable reality. I've mentioned before that Walt Disney said his greatest accomplishment was "building this organization, and *keeping it together*".

As is the case with many great leaders I've known or read about, Walt demanded *loyalty* from his key people. Here was the problem. Wood had developed *his* team within the Disney framework, a threat reminiscent of Walt's Oswald the Lucky Rabbit experience, when his creation, and team, were stolen from him. He had known his studio and WED people for years. And here was a new group of people who owed their loyalty to Wood; a team within his team.

There was a sadness about a change as major as this one. Instead of Woody's office being jammed with people looking for favors or decisions, people stayed away.

On Wood's last day, I suggested to Jack Sayers that we buy him a farewell drink. His office was almost empty when we arrived, and Wood was looking pensively out the window. Napoleon leaving for Elba.

He was glad to join us for a drink, which became several. He would move on to other projects, and I would be involved in some of them.

Walt acknowledged Wood's contributions, and he gave him a generous severance check.

It was the end of an era, the Wood Era, in the development of Disneyland.

One of my associates was a crusty man named Jim D'Arcy. He was a food specialist responsible for the Hills Brothers restaurant on Town Square. "What surprises me, " Jim commented, "is that the Disney Studio people have moved in so fast. All of the mistakes have not yet been made."

While Wood was in power, having a Texas accent was "in". It's only my guess, but Walt may have felt that he was being invaded by newcomers from the Lone Star State. Fortunately, some of the best Texans remained, because they had been carefully selected and were very sharp. And they adapted by dropping their typical Texas expressions and accents...at least when Walt was around.

Doc Lemmon and Howie Vineyard survived the Texas massacre, and George Whitney went to the defense of another Amarillo man who survived: Charley Thompson. Charley had two strikes against him. Not only was he a Texan, but he was also fat, and he told me that "Walt doesn't like fat guys." On the other hand, he was not only an outstanding finance man, but he had a great way of working with people and was a damned good showman. He had been the first manager of Adventureland and Frontierland, which were the best shows in the park.

It was the end of the Wood Era, an important period in bringing Walt's dream into reality. We aircraft people might have said that the "experimental plane was off the ground". The show people knew that it was going to be a success. Wood made his departure gracefully, and was already planning other theme parks which he would produce.

And, not for the first time in my career, I was wondering what would happen to *me*.

TWENTY-FOUR

I Get a New Boss

Wood's last day had been a Friday. I was without a boss.

That Sunday, Jack Sayers called me at home. The essence of our discussion, perhaps diluted over the years, was this: "Walt just called me at home. He asked me to take over Woody's job. I knew there was just one answer, and I said 'yes'." I extended my congratulations and suggested that we meet for a drink at the Stuft T-Shirt, a friendly Newport Beach bar.

It turned out that Jack was going to need a staff assistant and asked me if I wanted that job. And *my* answer was an immediate 'yes'."

Jack sold Walt on taking me on as his staff assistant. It was an easy transition for me, and I even got a $25 a week raise out of it. Walt said to Jack, and Jack said to me, that "We are not ready for a general manager with one man in control. We're still learning how to run the place."

I was also told that he said, "We're going to *operate* Disneyland at the park, but we're going to *manage* it from the studio."

Walt created a system of checks and balances which would continue for three decades. It was a unique plan for a unique organization.

Some of these changes are now taken for granted. They are a tribute to Walt's genius in organization. The Committee Operation Plan, with minor adaptions, remains today.

In effect, what Walt did was to take back full control of the park with a committee structure which would feed him information with which to make any final decisions.

It is always difficult to explain how any company really works, and we needed some kind of chart to explain how things worked. Knowing, fortunately, of Walt's aversion to organizational charts, I came up with one which was certainly not sophisticated, but gave most of us a fair idea of how we worked together.

Perhaps because it was not sophisticated, Walt approved it for our *Disneylander* house organ. And most certainly it explained in the center that Walt Disney was the Head Man of the Park...and don't you forget it!

Larry Tryon was the studio controller on loan to Disneyland as a finance director and a member of the committee.

Larry did not fit Walt's description of finance people being "sharp pencil guys". Larry was friendly, helpful, and creative. He had to be creative to juggle the income and expenses of our pioneering days. He always had time to explain finances to dummies like me. Larry kept a jar of nuts on his desk, with the Brazil nuts on the top. The message was: "The big ones always reach the top." He was thinking of hard work, not nutty folks.

One time he also demonstrated his ability to see into the future. Over drinks he said, "Van, today Disneyland is just the tail on the studio dog; at some point, the situation may be reversed." After about 20 years, Larry's prediction was proven to be right. For years, Disneyland and the other attractions have brought in more money than all studio productions.

The minutes of the Park Operations Committee meetings were always sent to Walt, but nobody knew whether he read them. I had my day when the committee found he *did* read them. I had sent in a request to entertain the wives of the Highway Patrol men at their annual meeting. I had asked for coffee and doughnuts and a ride on the *Mark Twain*. I had a reputation for being soft and "giving the park away". Jack, happily, told me that the committee had turned down my request.

A few days later, he got a call from Walt's secretary at the studio, who said: "Walt wants you to know that when his crews go out to location, the Highway Patrol is very helpful. He wants you to take care of the Highway Patrol wives, and their husbands, in any possible way."

We ended up taking the cast of the Golden Horseshoe Revue for a special show to the final meeting of the Highway Patrol. The committee had discovered that Walt *did* read the minutes, and I felt smart as hell.

TWENTY-FIVE

The Jack Sayers Era

I was moved from the White House to a small office in the old Dominguez home. It had been either a child's room or a large closet, but it *was* an office. I even acquired a secretary with a small staff to help me with a variety of new duties. In addition to orientation and leadership training, I became involved in a variety of new functions.

Jack's strength was in marketing, which he had learned when he worked with the Gallup Opinion Poll. That was where he had met Walt when he was handling movies for the now defunct *Look* magazine. He came up with the idea of polling our guests to find out where they came from and how they liked Disneyland.

I hired two competent, independent women who joined me as apprentices in Disneyland's first market research. Working with our advertising agency, they were dispatched to various areas of Los Angeles to find out which economic groups were our primary audience. The results showed that we had an *elite audience*, people from the middle- and upper-level income areas.

The area around Disneyland, which Walt would later call a "cheap Las Vegas strip", was what we called the "periphery property". Jack asked me to make a study of his area before it became populated by cheap motels and coffee shops.

I came up with a concept. I wanted to turn all the surrounding property into "The Disneyland Recreation Area", with coordinated building restrictions and signs, just like a national park.

Unfortunately, at that time some motels and restaurants had signs with names which infringed on Disney characters, and the Legal Department sued them to change any name which sounded like Disney, killing the concept.

Although my Disneyland Recreation Area idea died before it was born, I still think it would have prevented the cheap development that came later. And, by this time, I knew all the key people within the park and the community, which was essential to getting things done.

During our trial-and-error period, we had to find new ways to cope with a wide variety of problems. Certain memories come to mind:

Walt's Apartment

Everyone was curious about Walt's apartment located above the Fire Station on Main Street. So, for a re-orientation group I was leading, I managed to borrow a key (I can't remember how) and each group would "ooh" and "aah" as we walked through Walt's private quarters.

Many cast members enjoyed the tour until, on a rainy day, the raincoat of one participant brushed against one of Lillian Disney's table decorations. The cast member made a courageous reach, and fortunately caught it before it hit the floor.

In addition to the re-orientation traffic, a young host, the son of one of our executives, had found a key to the rooms, and had used the apartment for romantic purposes. I planned to have someone clean and straighten up, but I had somehow forgotten about it—a fatal error—just before Walt's weekend visit.

When the Housekeeping hostess entered the apartment in anticipation of Walt's arrival, she found clues that there had been unauthorized intruders. Panic buttons were pushed from Disneyland to the studio to WED and back.

That was the end of our tours of the apartment.

And It Isn't 5/8 Scale

During the orientation, we'd always said that Disneyland was designed to 5/8 scale, just to make it an easier size for children.

I included this in one of my handbooks, which Walt actually read. He immediately called Dick Irvine, the boss of WED, who called me and, in no uncertain terms, informed me that Disneyland was created in many different scales, to make the best effect.

The Spring Tonics of 1958

Old-timers still remember what we called the Spring Tonics. Although it was fun, it was also a serious attempt to improve morale by bringing some serious problems out in the open and laughing about them.

An informal opinion poll and my grapevine assured me that any standard motivational program would be called management bull. At the time, we had all of our meetings in the Mickey Mouse Theatre in Fantasyland. One of my union friends, hearing about the meeting, said: "What is this, another brainwash in the Mouse House?"

I turned to Wally Boag for help, and he brought in the Golden Horseshoe Revue, wrote the script, and trained our volunteer actors.

A review of the skits of the show is a partial summary of the "state of Disneyland morale" at that point in the history of the park.

Management understands...and has a sense of humor

Jack Sayers agreed to open the show with a planned gag. As he approached the microphone, the assembled audience expected a dull talk. Instead, Trinidad, our professional White Wing, entered the stage with his usual implements to follow the horses. We had to pay him overtime to get him to do it. But as he began sweeping around the mike, the audience cheered. Trinidad was a star. He wanted to stay on the stage and hear the applause. Jack finally had to push him off. From that first performance, Trinidad was right there for *every* performance...at straight pay.

Security officers were rude

At that time, our security force had a definite military posture. Frank Heidemann, the head of Security, was a ham at heart and agreed to do a skit mocking the attitudes of his officers. He played a new host who encountered a security officer with a gun. The officer made him place his hands against the wall...German concentration camp style. More huge applause.

Favoritism was rampant

Of course there was, and always will be, favoritism. But at the time many felt that it was either "who you know" or "how good looking you are". In the skit making fun of this problem, Wally Boag was shown hiring one of the Golden Horseshoe dancers, jumping over his desk to offer her a job.

Parking was hell

Employee parking will always be a problem. Guests get priority. It can be a long walk from car to work location. So we had a parking lot host dressed in a safari suit staggering around and crying, "Water...water!" That got another huge laugh.

Orange ties were hated

Doc Lemmon told me that Walt complained he could never find a supervisor when he wanted one. Doc came up with the idea for all supervisors to wear orange ties. On the basis of past experience, I thought it was a dumb idea. You can have a hundred good supervisors, but all you need is one miserable jerk and then all the others are tarred with the symbol. Orange ties had come to represent a miserable, "Peeping Tom" type of supervisor. Fortunately, even the supervisors hated those damned ties, or we might not have gotten away with our last skit. Close to the finale, one of our supervisors volunteered to come on stage with a huge, three-foot long, orange tie and a gorilla head we had borrowed from Wardrobe. Now *that* brought down the house.

The Parking Lot Olympics

When you work in hot weather, rain, fog, and smog, and you're dodging cars and answering interminable questions, you can almost lose your sanity.

The parking lot people are a tightly knit group. It's not a glamorous job, and it's seldom recognized by the press. But the cast members who work here usually have the highest morale of any in the park, and they have their own ways of preserving their sanity.

One of these sanity savers was the Parking Lot Olympics, an annual event approved by supervision. There was tough competition in several events involving those essential orange cones. Contests included:

- Cone Stacking: stacking the most cones in five minutes
- Cone Laying: proving speed and dexterity by laying cones in a line
- Cone Tossing: testing accuracy and distance by tossing cones like Frisbees
- Cone Skiing: standing on the cone and being towed; the longer, the better

Perhaps no other role can be as boring as parking lot cast member, and various stunts were pulled to make the job more interesting.

I like this story so well I've never told it until the participants were long gone.

It was in the early 1960s when yellow Volkswagens were a preferred mode of transportation. One frustrating day, the parking folks directed *all* yellow Volkswagens to the same section. Some of the culprits stayed around on their own time to enjoy the search when the owners returned and tried to find their own yellow bugs.

During what I call the Sayers Era, some of the progressive things we initiated would become permanent, although more sophisticated. Another metamorphosis in the organization was inevitable, but it came as a surprise.

Jack was called to the studio for a meeting with Card Walker, Vice President of Marketing. I was waiting at the Gourmet Bar at the Disneyland Hotel for his report. I was joined by Howie Vineyard in an informal corner of the bar. Jack arrived at about six, looking beat. After two vodka and tonics, he gave us the report. It was a bit ego-busting...

Jack was to be replaced as chairman of Park Operations by Joe Fowler. He was be assigned a new job as director of Lessee Relations.

Howie turned around and got sick. I had another drink and tried to be sympathetic while looking at the bright side.

Although there is no way to reduce the shock of being moved out of a top position, it was really a good move for Jack—and for Disneyland. Jack was a terrific salesman, and he was being placed by Walt where he could bring many institutional lessees into the park. Joe Fowler was a brilliant administrator who had earned Walt's complete confidence.

On about my third drink, a selfish thought came to mind: what would happen to *me*?

Once again I was a man without a boss. And this time the transition ended with a complete change in my Disneyland life.

TWENTY-SIX

Quitting Disneyland Is Hard to Do

An unusually long memo came out from Walt announcing that Joe Fowler was appointed vice president and chairman of the Park Operations Committee. Jack would be director of Lessee Relations, as I already knew, and other management changes were announced and confirmed. I can assure you that my name wasn't even mentioned, nor had Joe indicated that he needed a staff assistant.

From a purely practical viewpoint, I was in need of a new boss. I felt like an aging baseball pitcher about to be traded to a new team. Nobody really knew what the hell to do with me. I might have retreated to the protection of Fred Schumacher, but he considered training a necessary evil, and not nearly as important as his domain, the warehouse. Most of my functions seemed to fit in best with Tommy Walker's department, called—at that time—Customer Relations. It was agreed that I'd be moved under Tommy.

The new assignment started out well. Tommy was enthusiastic and had some great ideas. I brought added functions to his empire, particularly training, communications, and guest opinion polls. My enthusiasm began to unravel when he revealed his ambitious ideas for my orientation program. The plan was to get a stage with some props. Then, as conceived, I was to get up and give my presentation in a Mickey Mouse hat—the "Ears", as we call them. Although I admit to being a ham while giving "the pitch", Tommy's idea was just not my style. I never *talk down* to any group.

I may do some cheerleading, but I try to make it practical. I believe that a cast member who washes dishes *is* important, because he or she can prevent food poisoning. I try to give an honest pitch.

And since I hadn't been hired by Tommy, I wasn't really one of *his* team. This was not a good situation for me. Whenever he saw me talking to someone in another department, Tommy would want to know, "What were you talking to him about?" Although I was now solidly on the payroll, with a good track record and no fear of getting fired, an insidious little thought was creeping into my mind.

QUIT?

That little monster was the idea of *quitting*. Quitting Disneyland is hard to do.

It's a bit like quitting the Vatican. People wonder what's wrong with you. After all, most people *want* to work in the Magic Kingdom. And they might suspect that you quit because you were going to be fired.

My wife pointed out certain practical reasons not to quit, as wives will do:

- I was getting a regular paycheck. I was making house payments on time and paying off past debts.
- Although minimal by today's standards, the group insurance and other benefits were good.
- I would no longer be able to get jobs and passes for friends and relatives.

There was also the problem of leaving some good friends. At Disneyland, our friends are usually the people we work with. And most of us have been told that "quitters are always losers". I'm sure that some people felt I should see a psychologist. Yet I had quit other jobs when people thought I was crazy to do so, and I had always survived. I knew I would *not* be happy working for Tommy and his tight little group.

Wood had moved on and was promoting himself on his own as "The Master Planner of Disneyland", and had finally sold a contract for a theme park in Wakefield, Massachusetts. It had the not-too-original name of Pleasure Island, from the Pinocchio story. Wood asked me to do a handbook for the park. It was an interesting moonlighting job. From 3,000 miles away, he made it sound so exciting that I wanted to get involved. Also, Wood had recruited some ex-Disneyland friends whom I knew and liked, including Earl Shelton.

At about this time, Walt was getting testy about hearing Wood called "The Master Planner of Disneyland". He brought suit against Wood to cease and desist. Obviously, I couldn't continue to moonlight for Wood and stay at Disneyland. It was decision time. At one point in my past, I had quit a job when I didn't have another one lined up...a very dumb thing to do. And now I didn't have that problem.

Earl Shelton, the first man I had met on the Disneyland site, met me at the Lancers Bar, across from Disneyland. We had drinks together. Then, in Wood's name, he offered me $60 per day to work for Pleasure Island. I turned in my resignation to Disneyland the next day.

I gave Tommy my two weeks' notice. He was gracious about it, but I didn't get a chance to loaf. In fact, I worked overtime on a special project. Walt had been made chairman of the Pageantry Committee for the Winter Olympics of 1962, and Tommy was put in charge of the project. I was in an office behind his in City Hall, and we spent my last days developing the organization plan for the event. I missed those Olympics, but I always felt I had had a piece of the action.

If I had been fired, I probably would have received severance pay of a couple of weeks. But as a crazy person who quit, I got paid for my accrued vacation and I worked up till my last day.

And there was no farewell party. Jack and other friends took me out to lunch, a very wet lunch. There were no tears, but a lot of laughs.

Then I packed up for a new experience in Massachusetts.

PART THREE

Outside the Berm

1960–1962

TWENTY-SEVEN

Off to Boston

Leaving Disneyland was traumatic, but in reality I never did get far away. Although I had moved 3,000 miles to the East Coast, I was immediately surrounded by ex-Disneylanders.

Cliff Walker had been one of the first working foremen on the Jungle Cruise, under Dick Nunis. He was a natural showman with a philosophical bent and a sense of humor for the tough times of pre-openings. During one particularly hectic and frustrating day, he asked me, "Van, don't you wish you could just curl up in your mother's arms and tell her your troubles?"

Gene Johnson was a bright, wiry Swede who had been supervisor of Operations in Fantasyland. He was the only one of us who had brought his family along—his wife, Freda, and two charming kids. We ended up renting a mansion on Boston Bay, with Freda as the house mother for us itinerant consultants, and the kids making it feel like home.

Wood had sold the idea of Pleasure Island to the investors on the basis of Disneyland's figures. Unfortunately, they did not have the southern California climate, and they didn't have Walt. A few memories of my Pleasure Island experience pop up like mushrooms after the rain:

From White House to Tent Meetings

I was unable to find a building for orientation training. As a result, I set up training in a tent. The only problem was that it could get very hot—or, when the winds came, people would cringe from fear, expecting the tent to collapse.

We could cope by making the training an adventure...and fun. The theme was "It's Been My Pleasure", and we used the logo of a giant, smiling whale.

The Whale That Dived...Once

The symbol for Pleasure Island was a beautiful whale, which was used in all advertising and promotion.

The Big Show was to be the descent of the whale into a little lake, and it would then come up to spout and be cheered by the guests. Unfortunately, on its first test dive, the whale descended, but it never got back up from the bottom. It was resurrected to be seen, but it never worked.

Picnic and Weather

We didn't know that New Englanders demanded picnic areas around their amusement parks. We hadn't planned for that.

And we weren't ready for New England weather, and not for the local attitude about the weather: "If you don't like the weather, wait 15 minutes."

You Can Take the Boys Out of Disneyland, But...

When I was leaving Disneyland in 1959, plans were in progress for what Walt called "The Second Opening". This was to be what he had planned for the first opening...not the disaster which really took place in 1959.

We at Pleasure Island were all working 14 hours a day, seven days a week. But on a Sunday in June, Wood, Gene, Cliff, Earl, and I took the afternoon off to meet in my motel. We simply had to see what was the greatest spectacular TV program up to that time.

We wished we were there. We cheered. We felt part of it. It was the New Tomorrowland, the Submarine Voyage, the Monorail, the Matterhorn, and the new Autopias. Vice President Nixon cut the ribbon.

Although we were *physically* in a motel in Wakefield, Massachusetts, our hearts were still at Disneyland. After the show, we turned to beer and poker, and I lost. Fortunately, Wood let me put it on my expense report.

Wood's Champagne Fountain

The opening of Pleasure Island went well; attendance was good. To celebrate, Wood and about eight of us went out to dinner.

And to Wood, a time for celebration meant a time for his special Champagne Fountain. I was amazed as Wood carefully placed each of our champagne glasses one on top of another.

Then, as all of us and the restaurant staff watched, he poured champagne into the top glass, which overflowed down into the next one, and so on.

But this time, at precisely the wrong moment, my nervous leg kicked the table. Glasses and champagne spilled everywhere. Wood, with superb aplomb, merely asked the waiter for more glasses and champagne, and then said, "Van, you sit back from the table."

That...is real class!

Freedomland

While we were operating Pleasure Island, Wood was spending most of his time in New York wheeling and dealing to develop a new theme park in the Big Apple.

As soon as Pleasure Island closed for the summer, Wood immediately called me to New York. When Fred and I walked into his Manhattan hotel room, he pointed to a table where there was...a check for 13 million dollars!

Our Texas boss, who still used "Y'all" and "sodee pop", had sold the money men and real estate operators on the Freedomland park. The three of us just sat and stared at a check for that much money.

Unfortunately, the project was already off to a poor start. Unlike Walt, Wood wasn't too particular about the land for his park. One way he'd sold the project was by using some low-cost landfill acreage in the Bronx. When pile drivers would pound down great poles for foundations, the poles would simply disappear. Wood commented, "This is the last time I'll ever build a park on a thousand old gin bottles."

As at Disneyland, the black top for Freedomland was one of the last pre-opening projects. But at Freedomland, underneath the black top were mattresses, and mattress springs. These springs popped up through the black top, and I—as well as many guests—tripped over the hazards.

Eventually, money was in such short supply that Freedomland couldn't pay its tax bills. It was the beginning of the end.

Woody had invaded New York, but Freedomland would eventually die.

Being an itinerant consultant has its problems, but in spite of the frustrations, insecurity, and hectic schedules, the experience had been educational...and fun.

People complain about New Yorkers and New Englanders being cool and unfriendly, but I'd found just the opposite. I made good friendships which lasted for years.

But now it was time to leave, and Wood took some of us out for a farewell dinner.

Then I was headed back to California, without a job, without a client, and wondering what would happen next in my life.

The Graveyard of Theme Parks

I don't think there was anything called a *theme park* before Disneyland. Walt, or somebody, came up with the term to distinguish it from an "amusement park" or a "kiddie park". Further, it made sense. The THEME was *Walt Disney* and *Disney* history.

After the proven success of Disneyland, the copy cats of promotion and marketing adopted the "theme" for many ventures. There had been a few "lands" before Disneyland, such as Marineland, but now the term began to be used freely, and even for stores such as MattressLand, AutoLand, and ShoeLand.

There were early deaths, including Pleasure Island and Freedomland. Pacific Ocean Park in Santa Monica received financial transfusions for three years. The ocean survived; the park died.

And there was Bible Land. To be located on a lonely stretch on the way to Las Vegas, it would adapt some of Disneyland's concepts. The Peter Pan attraction would be converted to a ride through heaven. The cars would be formed like clouds. There would be angels. The Snow White attraction would be adapted for a struggle between David and Goliath. And instead of hamburgers, there would be *lionburgers*.

It never got off the ground, let alone the earth. Only the promoters and the artists who did the renderings made any money.

Other pseudo-theme parks died early, mostly because they were planned solely to make a fast buck. The promoters and builders of these parks forgot that Walt Disney created Disneyland as a work of love, not as a means to make a fortune. I believe that!

TWENTY-EIGHT

Back on My Own

When I tell career-minded young people that "it's not what you know but who you know", they think it is the cynical ramblings of an old man.

In my case, however, the only job I had ever gotten without some help from a friend was picking peas in Puyallup, Washington. I was too old for pea picking.

With this in mind, I had purposely kept in touch with my West Coast contacts while I was in the East. Further, as hundreds and maybe thousands of ex-Disneylanders have found, just mentioning that you've worked at Disneyland helps a lot.

As a result, I was soon involved in a network of consulting jobs which eventually led to some extensive work for the city of Costa Mesa, a young city which was trying to shake the image of "Goat Hill" to become "Angora Heights".

As luck would have it, Costa Mesa City Manager Bob Unger was a young man I'd met while I was doing a consulting job for UCLA. He had been the employment manager for a television manufacturing company. Bob was a creative thinker, and working with him was fun and a constant challenge to *my* creative thinking. We made a deal for half my time on a regular basis. And Bob landed me other assignments for reports and handbooks.

Bob had read an article in which a prestigious city planner had written, "Disneyland is the perfect design for a community." So why not use the concept for Costa Mesa. We spent many pleasant days designing the city of the future like Disneyland. A train would run around the town, there would be a Town Square, and there would be five separate neighborhoods, just as there were "lands" in Disneyland.

The mayor of the town and the councilmen enjoyed taking junkets to foreign lands. When they were asked, "Where is Costa Mesa?", they would reply, "South of Los Angeles," and they'd often be asked, "Where is that?" Finally, they had business cards printed with "Costa Mesa...just 16 miles west of Disneyland." That was immediate identification.

Things were going well. The Costa Mesa City Hall was only five minutes from my home office. And the city paid me right on time, which is important to a consultant. I was even considering a job as the manager of the local Chamber of Commerce when I received a call from Joe Fowler.

After a few pleasantries, Joe invited me to lunch...which turned out to be another life-changing event in my Disneyland career.

TWENTY-NINE

A Luncheon Deal

Joe and I met for lunch at the Oak Room in the Disneyland Hotel. The Oak Room was a semi-private club. Since I knew the manager, bartender, and, most important, the waitress, I felt right at home.

On a person-to-person basis, Joe Fowler is one of the most charming individuals I've ever met. We had a conversational bridge based on our wives' mutual friendship. They shared the same church work and the same therapist. I'm sure they spent many hours together, complaining about their husbands who were married to their work.

After the pleasantries, Joe got right to the reason for the lunch. Morale at the park was low and something needed to be done. We were getting more guest complaints about poor service than in the past.

He brought me up to date on a major organizational change at the park which I had already heard about when I attended a farewell party for Doc Lemmon. Doc had resigned to become vice president of Cedar Point Resort in Ohio. Dick Nunis had been selected to replace him as director of Operations.

Then, getting back to the point, Joe asked if I would be interested in coming back to Disneyland on a consulting basis. I told him that I *was* interested. Joe coughed a couple of times and brought up the subject of money. Bob was paying me $300 a week, but I upped that amount by $100, knowing that Joe wouldn't check it out. Joe felt that if a little city called "Goat Hill" could pay me that amount, Disneyland certainly could match it.

Joe pointed out that I wouldn't be reporting to him. I would be working for Dick Nunis, my former gofer. Dick is not the type of person who takes credit for helping other people. And to this day, I've never asked him how it was arranged that I was called back. Luncheon was over, and Joe is not the type to sit around for small talk. With a firm handshake, and his characteristic "CAN DO!", he returned to Disneyland.

Now I had a new worry. You've heard of *You Can't Go Home Again* by Thomas Wolfe? I was to learn that you *can* go home again...but it was going to be tough.

PART FOUR

Second Time Around

1962–1963

THIRTY

Re-Orientation, Nunis-Style

The first day on any job or new assignment is always tough. Reporting *back* to Disneyland was perhaps my most worrisome such experience.

First, there was a definite policy against rehiring anyone who had deserted the Magic Kingdom. It was a bit like a priest returning to the Vatican after leaving to marry a prostitute.

Second, I was going back to work for Dick Nunis, my former gofer, whom I had given a bad time when he first reported to me wearing suede shoes.

Third, by now I was pushing 50 years of age, an old person by Disneyland's youthful standards.

Dick had carefully planned my retraining program and took the time to personally introduce me to all the key people, although I knew many of them already. He outlined the problems as he saw them and showed that he was open to ideas and suggestions.

In addition, Dick recalled one of our rambling conversations from our White House days and reminded me of it. I had read an article about the way older people dressed. The article stated that young people, being young and naturally good looking, spent too much money on their clothes. Older people, sagging and stooping a bit, didn't spend enough. And now, Dick Nunis began a personal grooming program for me, which I remember vividly and try to follow to this day.

He insisted that I learn to tie a necktie. "You're still using that old-fashioned four-in-hand knot," he said. "You have to get with it and learn the Windsor knot." For two weeks I had to practice at home the modern way of tying my damned tie. He finally approved my proficiency.

Dick also checked the rest of my attire. I *had* become a bit seedy. Once he caught me wearing a shirt with a frayed collar. "Damn it, Van, you make enough money to buy a decent shirt," he told me. "Don't let me see you with an old shirt." I didn't take him seriously enough.

At one time, when Dick had approved my hiring a new person, he admonished me with "now don't train *him* like you did *me*". I'll admit that I'd just thrown him in to those turbulent pre-opening waters and let him "sink or swim" on his own. He swam.

His program for me was much more than needling and grooming. It reflected sensitivity and genuine concern for my survival. He knew I was insecure about returning, and there were probably some people who hadn't approved my being rehired.

My orientation was thorough. It included lunch in the executive dining room at the studio. As we left, I heard someone yelling, "Hey, Van!" I looked around. It was Walt. He welcomed me back. And then he said, "I'll bet you learned a lot while you were away." I responded that I certainly had learned a lot...and that was as honest a statement as I could make.

Walt's comment about my learning in the outside world helped me. I could now look at Disneyland with fresh insights.

Dick's well-planned and totally understanding program has stuck with me throughout the rest of my life. And thanks to Dick, my orientation helped me feel "back at home". My ties were all tied, and my shirts had no holes.

I was ready to start my second time around at Disneyland.

THIRTY-ONE

"Tijuana Row" Days

Upon my return in 1962, the Operations offices were located in a group of pre-opening construction shacks aptly named "Tijuana Row" (aptly named because they looked like a shanty town, not much different from the run-down shacks that at the time were prevalent in Tijuana, just over the border with Mexico).

Dick Nunis and Bob Reilly had offices, but the rest of us, including secretaries and managers, worked out of one large room. I don't think I even had a desk.

It was primitive, but it was also vibrating with activity. It was communal. People had to get along with each other. I'm sure Walt liked it, since these surroundings were neither fancy nor expensive.

In the early days, somebody tried to sell Walt on an administration building. He turned it down. "First, I don't want to spend money on something the guests can't see," he said, "and second, people will stay in their offices when should be out in the park making sure things run right."

Walt was absolutely correct. An office and a desk can be protection from the heat or the cold. In Tijuana Row, we certainly used any excuse to get out into the park. Besides, if Dick saw us just sitting in the office, he might kick us out.

Perhaps the reason Dick brought me back was that the person who took over training when I left was not in touch with how the people who operated the park were thinking.

Bud Coulsen was a competent radio and public relations man. Unfortunately, he continued to preach "happiness" to the people who were fighting for work hours, doing tough job, and working strange shifts at Disneyland. What he was selling, the people weren't buying.

As you must know by now, the "good old days" were not all that good. Yet there had been an excitement and romance about them. There was something new every day and not too many rules and regulations. The rapid growth of the park changed that. Now, we *needed* policies, rules, and regulations, and lots of them. This was a sharp change from the ways of the past, and people resented the move away from the "trial-and-error" management they had grown up with.

Anyone who has ever been married knows there is a huge difference between the moonlight and roses of courtship and the bills and responsibilities of marriage. And, as in marriage, some people had sort of an occupational "seven-year itch". Many *did* leave, but others stayed around, unhappy with their work and themselves.

In addition, people working at Disneyland were often asked by friends and family, "When are you going to get a *real* job?" This continues today, even though Disneyland has been the best and most consistent employer in the area. But at the time I returned, many people were finding that they were married to Disneyland, and it was more than just a casual affair.

Whenever we would take over the contracts of our lessees, people would either be let go or transferred to the Disneyland payroll. This created the perfect climate for rumors...changes and insecurity. These rumors pervaded all levels. Managers wondered how they would survive the changes and had to adapt to new bosses.

By this time, we had decided to bring in extra supervision for what was then the big "harvest period" of summer. Some people, from the hourly ranks, would be selected for these jobs. For a time they wouldn't have to punch the clock. The could wear suits and ties. They would "move up" for a four-month period, and then they would be "dropped back" to wearing costumes and filling in time cards.

There were drawbacks to this "Yo Yo" supervision system:

There might be two people with equivalent education, experience, and performance. One would temporarily become the supervisor of the other, who was perhaps his buddy, even a fraternity brother. The other would feel rejected.

At the end of the summer, the "Yo Yo" would be stripped of his elevated responsibilities and privileges, and return to work with his fellow hourlies whom he had supervised for four months.

This practice may have been necessary, but it succeeded most in dampening morale and enthusiasm.

With the park's increase in size, some cast members would be promoted on a permanent basis, and other would not. There were also preferred jobs and preferred shifts. In the process of selecting who would fill the available slots, the cry of "favoritism" was a frequent criticism. People who tried to get along with management were accused of trying to collect brownie points.

Walt would regularly walk through the park, looking for problems or things to improve. He was good at it and always welcomed suggestions.

I copied his routine. I continually walked through the park, but looking for different things—*people problems*. Facts are easy to identify. I was looking for *feelings* that were bothering cast members.

I would never turn people off when they wanted to gripe or blow off steam. And more often than not, I agreed with the gripers, which did not endear me to their managers.

There was a definite reality gap between the romance we preached in orientation and the actualities of some jobs. A bright-eyed, young person would be told he was part of the cast of a beautiful Walt Disney show, and then would report to his work location where his hardened foreman would tell him a different story.

A cast member assigned to Autopia would hear "Blood Alley". That same cast member reporting to the Skyway might be shown how to operate "Hemorrhoid Hollow".

In orientation, we spent a great deal of time on our understanding of teamwork, although that concept was close to an outright lie. Our Maintenance and Operations people were particularly antagonistic toward each other. Maintenance referred to Operations as "button pushers", and Operations returned the compliment, calling Maintenance workers "bulb changers".

A caste system had developed, with some groups feeling they were better than others. (And the tour guides felt they were better than *everybody*.)

Strangely, nobody ever blamed Walt Disney for anything. He was everyone's hero. The primary object of their frustrations was "the management" or "those dumb supervisors", and it was true, we *did* have some supervisors who had no training or talent for leading people.

Things would have been much worse, in retrospect, if it hadn't been for my three heroines of Tijuana Row.

THIRTY-TWO

Three Heroines of Tijuana Row

During my absence, not much had been done to train our supervisors. I take that back. The basic instruction for young supervisors had been handled by three women in Tijuana Row.

Dorothy Eno

In my orientation, Dick had made it clear to me, abundantly clear, that if I didn't get along with his assistant, Dorothy Eno, I should be nice to Bob Unger (Costa Mesa's city manager) because I would be back working for him.

Getting along with Dorothy was easy to do, and our friendship continues even today.

I had met Dorothy in the early days when she was a secretary scrunched in with three supervisors in a little office above the shops in Adventureland.

She had survived the experience to become Doc Lemmon's secretary. To call her a secretary, or an executive secretary, or even a staff assistant, would not give full credit to her contributions to Disneyland. Dorothy had educated and protected Doc, and was now in charge of educating and protecting Dick. They had a close, unique working relationship. He looked to her and to Walt for guidance.

Behind her young, innocent face was a mind and memory equal to Dick's. Fortunately, for me, she took me on as a student.

For nearly 25 years I looked to her for counsel and advice. If she checked the copy of any of my handbooks, I knew it was OK. I learned to detect her rating plan. If my work was bad or just average, she'd look at me, and I knew it had to be redone.

Whenever Dick was traveling and not available on the spot, there was no problem in getting a decision. "Eno" had the answer, or she knew where to get it.

And when I went through a divorce and a death in my family—upsetting my work life, to say the least—Dorothy was right there to help me get over the rough spots.

Like me, Dorothy didn't believe in our fancy retirement parties. But she did allow Dick to give a small dinner when she finally retired, during which the drinks and tears flooded our private room.

Not only could Dorothy out-think any of us, she could out-drink any of us, too.

Carolyn Long

Also housed in those primitive surroundings was Carolyn Long. She had worked for George Mills, Sr., the superintendent of construction for Disneyland. George was from the "old school" of construction. Success in that school required many things not covered in MBA programs. George was excellent in bombast, threatening, yelling...and getting the job done. Anyone who could successfully work for George would have no trouble with the young, inexperienced men who were promoted to supervisor.

Irene Fleetwood

Irene Fleetwood, the third member of our supervisor training trio, was the youngest, and not exactly a threatening size. She was probably about 5'2" tall, pert, and refused to answer to the nickname "Bones". Although diminutive in size, she was not about to take any bull from any of these young men in their fancy shoes.

Many young supervisors owe their careers to these women who trained them—myself included. Anyone who ever thought about complaining to Dick about being cut down by Irene, Carolyn, or Dorothy could expect, at the least, a chewing out by Dick. In addition, he would probably end up on Dick's "non-exist" list, and should be looking for other employment.

Having been on the "outside", I was full of fresh ideas, and then I was a sponge for ideas and complaints from people in the park.

Dick would pick up on the ideas he thought would work and take action where it was justified. But he had a couple of ways of stopping me. One was to reach into his desk and pull out a crying towel which he would hand to me when I started to complain. Basic communications. Another was a large cardboard visual aid that he had Dorothy design for him. Before I would even open my mouth, he would haul out a sign which had just one word: NO!!

But then, one of the ideas Dick did buy became vital to my future and the future of Disneyland.

THIRTY-THREE

Birth of the University of Disneyland

Today, the University of Disneyland is a well-accepted part of the organization. In fact, we also have Disney University campuses at the studio, and at our theme parks in Florida, Japan, and France.

The concept of a university in a service industry has been adapted by others. McDonald's "Hamburger University" is one of the most extensive. Back in 1962, there were some who thought the idea was crazy. A "university" for an amusement park...you've got to be kidding!

But Ed Ettinger wasn't kidding when he planted the seed during a coffee break one day. Ed, who was the Public Relations director at the time, was a brilliant guy, and his observations went about like this:

"What we need is something that affects the total organization. Some tired training program won't do it. We need something like a university...a program which pioneers new ground in this revolutionary concept of Walt's."

But it took more than a good idea to bring the university into existence. This new baby in the corporate family might have died in the delivery room had it not been for certain circumstances.

First, I had an aversion to the concept of a "training department". The function has little status in any organization. Years before, when I had actually managed a "training department", I grew tired of hearing, "Those who *can*, do; those who *can't*, teach."

Further, any high school graduate feels that he or she has already been trained and resents being enrolled again. On the other hand, the idea of a *university* was exciting. Historically, a university was ahead of the times, leading people into exciting adventures—even student riots.

Second, Dick's degree from USC was in education, and he could see the advantages of branching out from a simple orientation program. When Dick buys an idea, he backs it and sells it.

"The University" was a good name. But would it have any substance in the organization?

Disneyland was a branch of show business, and Walt was the executive producer. But there were some who still thought of it as an "amusement park". There were still those inside and outside the organization who didn't think of our work as a real job. So, a basic goal of our university was to make working at Disneyland a new profession, a respected branch of show business. With pardonable pride, I feel we did a better job of pioneering the burgeoning service industry than any legitimate institutions of higher learning.

But we were starting from scratch, and since we were constantly short of money, we had to fight for even the most elemental things.

For example, there was no place for training in Tijuana Row, and the Mickey Mouse Theatre could no longer be used, as it was bringing in revenue. We needed a place of our own.

Dick and I shopped around on Harbor Boulevard and finally bought a trailer which would become the headquarters for the University of Disneyland. Even without ivy-covered walls, it became an institution of higher learning, a place for our people to come to training meetings.

Today, every office has computers able to display advanced visual aids. But when our university was beginning, we had to develop a major sales program to purchase one typewriter and one carousel projector for slides. In fact, ours was the *first* IBM electric typewriter at Disneyland.

We now had a building for our university, but we didn't have a staff of professors.

So we started the tradition of begging, borrowing, and stealing people from within the organization as part-time instructors. Fortunately, we needed people at the very times that attendance was slow, and they could be released from their regular jobs.

These people brought to the university a wealth of practical experience, and it was good exposure and learning for them, as well.

The idea of a Disneyland University was not an instant success. There were those who associated the term "university" with professors in ivory towers removed from the realities of life. Many preferred the safe sound of a "Training Department", instead.

But when Walt Disney mentioned "our university", the idea got its official approval.

Finally, we were getting some respect.

- -

The Four Keys

Dick came up with a program which could have been called "Introduction to Professional Theme Park Operation". To help get the message across, it was titled "Safety... Courtesy...Show...Capacity".

At the time, it was a totally new concept for Operations. The four elements, or keys, or theme park operations were listed in their order of importance:

- *Safety.* When guests come to Disneyland, they put their safety in Walt Disney's hands.

- *Courtesy.* We represent the entire Disney organization in the guests' person-to-person contact with us.

- *Show.* Disneyland is a spectacular show, and we are show people. We may work "on stage" or "backstage", but all our efforts combine to create the world's greatest show.

- *Capacity.* We have a limited capacity. Every seat must be utilized. (We later changed this key to "Efficiency".)

- -

THIRTY-FOUR

The University Branches Out

Our university absorbed all the training and human relations functions which had been ongoing during my absence, including the *Disneylanders* house organ and the Disneyland Recreation Club. In addition, the advantage of having a "University" instead of a "Training Department" was that we could branch out into any area of human relations or communications.

Prior to starting at Disneyland in 1955, I had worked with UCLA in conducting confidential employee opinion polls. I'd found that these were effective in finding problems affecting the organization. We made a contract with CalTech to conduct our first Disneyland poll.

This poll gave cast members a chance to express their frustrations, and we identified problems we had only suspected. There were the usual comments about favoritism and supervision (too many chiefs and not enough Indians...and *dumb* chiefs, at that).

We would also determine real problems which could be corrected. For example, we found that there was a universal frustration with our locker rooms, break rooms, and cafeteria. At a cost of nearly $500,000, we improved these areas. And with a follow-up opinion poll, we found that the complaints were reduced by 80%.

But there were then, as there are today, some problems for which there are no solutions, such as parking, security, scheduling, and grooming. I sold Dick on the idea that we should spoof the problems in an employee publication and let people know that we realized these problems existed.

Wally Boag, the top banana of the Golden Horseshoe, volunteered to be editor. His gag writer was a clerk in the Plumbing Department whose name was...honestly...Claude Plumb.

With some help from an artist, we produced a dummy which let all the problems see the light of day. We spoofed WED, the studio, ourselves. It was sort of a Disney *MAD Magazine*, and we called it *Backstage Disneyland*.

Dick worried about it, but he carried around the dummy of that publication until he could show it to Walt. Walt understood the reason for it, and gave his OK. And then, if someone complained, we would say, "Walt liked it...so gripe to him." That took care of *that*.

There is the *calendar* year, and the financial folks have a *fiscal* year. At Disneyland in 1963, we had what I called the *morale* year.

Disneyland's attendance is seasonal in nature. During 1963 we had a total attendance of 5.6 million guests (less than half of what it would be 20 years later) and half of this number came during our "harvest season", the three months of summer.

There would be two "let-down" periods: the month after Labor Day and the months after New Year's. During these periods, cast members would be laid off or have their hours reduced. Fewer hours meant lower pay, and lower pay meant lower morale. These were times when the grapevine sprouted rumors, and the level of gripes and grievances was high. We tried to counteract these highs and lows by initiating a variety of programs.

The Canoe Races

To build morale during the summer when our younger staff was working, we came up with what are now our famous canoe races. Was there interest? Our people still come out at five in the morning to practice, before the park opens. (At that hour *I* have never participated.)

Disney Family Film Festival

It started out slow, but eventually we had a regular film series (free) for cast members and their families.

The Annual Christmas Party

This would become one of the great advantages of working at Disneyland. At the annual party, when the park was beautifully decorated, members of management would work and entertain the cast. Not that our key executives don't try, but we've had to add some experienced cast members to help train and supervise *them*.

Sports

Disneyland has a high percentage of jocks and ex-jocks. I'm not included, but we have a full complement of intra-functional teams which take these games very seriously.

Even with all these additional activities and benefits, however, it was time for a new theme which would motivate new hires as well as those already working for us.

THIRTY-FIVE

The Disneyland World Spectacular Show

It is always easy to motivate the new people in their first orientation. They are happy to have a job at Disneyland, and they are being paid. Unfortunately, they then go work with a peer group which has been around for a few years, and may have hardened attitudes.

Our White House theme of "happiness" was great for the first years, and we still use the basic elements of that program. But now we needed something new, something that would impose responsibility and self-discipline on all of our key people. Not for the first or the last time, cast members who had been around for a few years would say, "Don't give us that pixie dust."

And some of our more hard-nosed supervisors would complain that we were preaching "happiness" when the reality was that young people just needed more discipline.

I should mention that over the years I've heard, perhaps thousands of times, that "These young people today don't like to work any more!" and "Morale is lower than ever!" (a maxim which is repeated every year).

My answer to "Don't give us that pixie dust" was, and is, "Dammit, our product IS pixie dust!"

We were also fighting "amusement park thinking". Since I had heard it straight from Walt, I preached that Disneyland was NOT an amusement park.

So what was it? We came up with the concept that it was a "world spectacular show" played on a 74-acre stage with the southern California sky as a giant backdrop. We then compared this famous outdoor show with a theater, and came up with some concepts still alive and well today:

- Our *outer lobby* was the parking lot, where the experience must start on a friendly note.
- Our *inner lobby* was the main gate, that sensitive area where people were separated from their money.

- And then the *berm* acted as the outer walls for our spectacular show. Our guests who were our audience then walked through the stage entrance to our 74-acre stage.

- Our *"on stage" cast* mix and blend with our audience of guests. Food service, souvenir merchandising, operations, special shows, and custodial personnel are all essential to the perfect show.

- Our *backstage cast* included all of the technicians, craftsmen, and the many others who worked behind the scenes in offices.

Included in the presentation was the fact that we had a worldwide reputation for friendliness and cleanliness, and that Walt insisted that "the streets be clean enough to eat off of".

Dick approved the concept, but now the challenge was to sell it to all the members of what we were now calling our *cast*.

We found help where we needed it, from a unique crew of young people who were out there actually working the attractions, and who shared Walt's dream.

PEP, an acronym for Personnel Exposure Plan, gave me temporary staff help and exposed the talents of some of our young people to management. During the slow periods, as in May, we had no trouble borrowing people on the hourly payroll. Managers on tight budgets were happy to have the university absorb their hours. Some who were working on short hours were glad to increase their earnings, and I could hide many of the costs.

Our PEPster pool was full of hourly people who were bright, well-educated, and under-utilized. I fished around in this pool to find a group which could help me produce a good pre-summer motivational show. That first show was produced in the Mickey Mouse Theatre.

I always believe in dressing up an orientation room. I wanted the room to *feel* like show business. I call it "training by osmosis". We used canvas captain's chairs, each having a stencil of some movie star who had worked at Disneyland, and of course chairs for Walt and Roy Disney. One could sit where a famous star might have sat. We used the tops of large film cans for ash trays.

Today, the chairs are comfortable and the carpet beautiful, and there's a special area for projecting films. And nobody even *thinks* of smoking. Walt, a heavy smoker, would have had a tough time there.

Most of the elements of the spectacular show concept are still used. Selling pixie dust? You're damned right. That's what we do, and I'm proud of it.

THIRTY-SIX

New York World's Fair: 1964

The New York World's Fair of 1964 was in trouble. The Fair committee needed a master showman to bring life and excitement to a project which seemed a bit dull.

The promoters turned to Walt Disney, and he drove a hard bargain. He agreed to design four attractions, provided that he could bring them to Disneyland after the Fair closed:

- Great Moments with Mr. Lincoln debuted for the State of Illinois
- The Primeval World segment of the Disneyland Railroad was first produced for the Ford Motor Company's exhibit at the Fair
- The Carousel of Progress was designed for General Electric
- "it's a small world" was designed for the Pepsi-Cola Company

Disneyland was booming, and the Fair would require the talents of many of our key people. Our job was to train the 100-or-so New Yorkers who would need extensive orientation and training for the "it's a small world" attraction. In addition, there would be 450 part-time UNICEF volunteers. Pepsi had designated all proceeds to be donated to the worldwide children's relief fund. This would require that training and orientation go on nearly round-the-clock for about 30 days. I definitely needed help, and got some:

Ted Crowell didn't just accidentally end up at Disneyland. We recruited him when he graduated from Cal State San Luis Obispo as an industrial engineer, and he accepted a job working for Dick Nunis. Ted immediately showed his great worth by establishing a system for predicting attendance. He could predict how many hot dogs would be needed on any given day with only a 5% error. Since I needed a backup, Dick selected Ted, knowing it would be good experience for an engineer. It was. Ted soon learned how to give a motivational pitch.

Chuck Burns was a great balance for Ted and me. He was a perfect detail man, but he also knew show business from his days as a professional clown. He had also been a character at Disneyland (one of those in costume, not one of the strange types I've mentioned).

Bill Hoelscher, an ex-Jungle Cruise foreman and ex-PEPster, had been selected to be our key recruiter in New York. He told Dick that he was finding some good people, but since one of our ex-Disneylanders had told Dick that we wouldn't be able to find any "Disney types" in New York, Dick didn't take Bill's opinion at face value. He went through the area and helped interview. "Van," he said, "those other guys just didn't know how to pick them and train them." He was absolutely right. Thanks to him, the quality of our Pepsi cast was every bit as high as that of our Orange County people.

After designing and practicing the program, it was time to pack up our visual aids and move to New York. I left the university in the loyal hands of Gary Fravel, and he used the opportunity to build up our permanent staff.

Dick remembered how difficult it had been for us to find a place for orientation when Disneyland was under construction. So, a year before the Fair was due to open, he leased space for an orientation room in a motel which was just being built. It was a stroke of genius.

We didn't want some dull training room for sophisticated volunteers. To give our room some local class, we dressed it up like a New York café with checkered tablecloths, flowers, and a beautiful handbook as a menu.

We had over 500 people to orient, and we did it in groups of 20, a night and a day, seven days a week, groups assembly-style. Our New Yorkers, both those getting paid and the volunteers, became dedicated "Ambassadors of Happiness".

My wife and I had a room at our motel headquarters, and I would simply run downstairs to handle orientation. I stored materials in our room.

One day, a housekeeper asked me for a souvenir book to give her son, who was sick. That was easy. She also wanted the book autographed. I think you'll agree that my name wouldn't mean much. Since I'm pretty good at Walt's signature, I thought, just this once, I'd sign it. I wrote something like "Get well, Tom. Walt Disney."

It was like feeding pigeons. Soon every maid, waitress, and bartender had a sick child. I hope they saved these souvenirs with pride, signed, as far as they know, by a very famous man.

There were some in New York who, for varying reasons, fought against the World's Fair.

One rumor was that there would be a demonstration where hundreds of cars would be purposely stalled in all tunnels leading to the Fair, completely disrupting traffic. Another rumor was that there would be a demonstration in front of our UNICEF Pepsi attraction.

This was a challenge that Dick liked. He was prepared to convince those demonstrators that they should go elsewhere, that our attraction was helping starving children around the world.

And there *was* a demonstration. However, it was against a beer company exhibit next to ours. Nobody from the beer company spoke to the demonstrators, as Dick would have done. They simply called the police and had them hauled off to jail.

Despite these minor problems, opening day for "it's a small world" was great. Walt and the Pepsi-Cola president were there for the dedication. Tommy Walker put on a great show, complete with a balloon ascension.

Jack Sayers had warned me that Walt was in a bad mood, having real problems with Mr. Lincoln. It was a good time to stay out of his way, but my wife wanted me to introduce her. I explained to her why I didn't think it was a good idea, but the head of UNICEF said, "Come on, Patti, I'll introduce you," and he did. Patti was a naturally exuberant person and told Walt something like, "Those balloons were wonderful."

Walt was as polite as possible, but he was totally preoccupied, and he replied as he walked away, "Balloons are *always* good."

Considering the circumstances, it was a damned good training program. Pepsi was happy. UNICEF was happy. And our cast performed up to our Disneyland reputation for courtesy and efficiency. Unfortunately, I hadn't taken the time to involve Tommy Walker in my training program, which would have been the politically prudent thing to do. As a result, whenever anything went wrong that first year, he could blame the orientation program.

Dick also ended up with some bruises. He had been told to "take the ball and run", and when he does that, he charges as he did during his college football career. He received the blame for everything I, and anyone else, did wrong.

The World's Fair was an important step ahead for Disneyland and the future of the organization. We brought all of our attractions back to California. And both Dick and I learned that when you are told to "take the ball and run with it", you should not forget that you can be clipped from behind.

Dick left New York a week before we did. He allowed us to stay around for a week to close up our training program and enjoy a little of New York.

Then it was back to California and some new, unexpected experiences.

THIRTY-SEVEN

Disneyland's Vintage Years

When I returned from New York, Disneyland was jumping, with 1965 our tencennial year.

For those of us who had previously had our doubts about the success of Disneyland, the fact that Walt's dream was alive, and literally exploding, was a major event. It may seem strange for those who are now accustomed to an audience of 12 million to realize that our growth in attendance from 1.4 million the first year to 6.4 million the tenth year was a miracle.

And then there was *Mary Poppins*. This movie brought in more Academy Awards, and more money, than anyone, including Walt, had anticipated. Walt began pouring the Mary Poppins money into Disneyland. Although he was a true American patriot, he didn't enjoy sending taxes to be spent by government bureaucrats. He liked to use money to create new things at Disneyland, and explained it this way:

"Like the old farmer, you've got to pour it back in the ground if you want it to grow. That's my brother's philosophy and mine, too.

Construction at the park taking place then reminded me a bit of our pre-opening days. New Orleans Square, the Pirates of the Caribbean, and the Plaza Inn were all under construction, as was "it's a small world", the Carousel of Progress, the PeopleMover, and other new attractions.

The Tencennial Celebration was a year-long special event The *Disneyland* TV show had changed to *The Wonderful World of Color* and featured a salute to Disneyland, which helped to boost attendance.

With all the increased activity, the university was allowed to grow. I added more bright, young people to the staff, and we even had *two* secretaries.

Walt finally approved construction of an administration building. The idea was sold to him because there was an additional, practical reason for it. Joe Fowler explained to Walt that housing was needed for the Primeval World. The university ended up with some rather fancy quarters, although in the offices you could hear the rumbling of the *Santa Fe* train as it went past Tyrannosaurus Rex.

Mr. Lincoln was the first of the New York projects to be completely redone for Disneyland. Walt liked my handbook for the attraction, and a note from indicating his approval is one of my prized possessions.

Walt had carefully planned the opening of "it's a small world" to prevent a let-down after the Tencennial Celebration in 1965. We spent $6 million on the attraction when it was moved from New York to Disneyland. By the time of its opening, Jack Lindquist and his staff had become experts at staging special events. On this occasion, in addition to the band and the ribbons, there were bottles filled with water from lands around the world. The water was ceremonially poured into the boat channel during the celebration. I've *never* asked the true source of those waters.

For Walt, there was an important message in "small world". Children of all nations, creeds, and colors are happy together. It's the adults who mess things up.

Another addition to New Orleans Square was an exclusive restaurant, Club 33, primarily for V.I.P. executives and celebrities. It was adjacent to a new apartment being designed for Walt and Roy.

I've been asked why it was named with those numbers. Jack Olsen, who was on the planning team that went to the *real* New Orleans to research, told me there were many addresses with two numbers, and he couldn't remember why the number "3" was selected. But my guess is that Walt needed some more 3s to go with our 1313 Harbor address.

There was a policy problem with the club: booze. Some of these V.I.P. potential members who pay a good price to join would want a drink with lunch or dinner, and Disneyland was dry.

Dick tells the story of how he argued against allowing drinks in the club. He was one of the few who would argue with Walt, taking as he would say "only two strikes". After listening to Dick's objections, Walt declared that there would be no drinks. But later, he told Dick that if it was ever a problem, he'd change it. There's never been a problem.

With all of this frantic growth in 1965, one event stands out as the greatest celebration of Disneyland's early pioneers—a memorable night with Walt and Roy Disney.

THIRTY-EIGHT

The Big 10th Anniversary For Pioneers

On July 17, 1965, there was reason to celebrate. A party was planned for all the people who had been working at Disneyland in 1955...and were still working there.

Today, the pioneers of that opening year continue to get together on July 17. The reunions are limited to those who are still actively working. As a result, through death and retirement, the group is getting smaller every year. It is called Club 55, and it's as exclusive a group as you can find.

No meeting since then compares with that night of July 17, 1965. There were free drinks and great food, and a band for entertainment and dancing. Walt and Roy attended with their wives, and both were in great form.

As the finale, Jack Sayers introduced Roy and Walt and invited them to speak. Fortunately, somebody remembered to tape Walt's remarks. And even more important, we saved them.

It was Walt at his best, and his most candid, showing great humor and sharing insights into the history of Disneyland and predictions for its future. With only minor editing, here are some comments by Walt Disney on that night of July 17, ten years after Disneyland's opening:

Wally Boag

"I had a little interview over at the studio. In came this fellow. He had a little bag with him, and in the bag he had a dummy. And he had some other things. He had some bagpipes. He came on the stage all alone.

"And I said, 'Well, we're trying to put a little show together. You know this Disneyland, it's going to be a family place.' And he said, 'Well, I have some routines I've been doing in night clubs, but I can clean 'em up.'

"And he cleaned 'em up, you know. But I think there's just a little hangover in a few of those jokes, but it slips by and nobody realizes it. That was Wally Boag, and Wally, I hope you've been happy and stay with us."

Disneyland Problems

"Well, we had a lot of problems putting this thing together. There was pressure for money. A lot of people didn't believe in what we were doing. And we were putting the squeeze play where we could.

"I remember that we were dealing with all three networks. They wanted our television show. And I kept insisting I wanted an amusement park. And everybody said, 'What the hell's he want that damn amusement park for?' And I couldn't think of a good reason except, I don't know, I wanted it.

"ABC needed the television show *so damned bad* that they bought the amusement park, too."

Buying Out ABC

"Well, five years later, my brother figured we better buy those guys out. They had a third interest. They only had a half-million dollars invested in that park. He figured, 'If we don't buy 'em out now, we're gonna be payin' a lot more later.' My brother paid them, after five years, seven-and-a-half-million dollars for their investment. And it was a smart move that he did that."

Fighting the Bankers

"Well, my brother has had the worries of getting this money and fighting the bankers and things. And there was a time, I think it was after we opened the park, that our bankers said to my brother, 'Now about that damn amusement park, we're not gonna let you put another nickel in it.' And my brother said, 'Well, if you're gonna start running our business, we're going out and we'll find some other place we can borrow money.'

"And by gosh, they finally gave him the money."

They Got Wise

"But it's been nip and tuck. I mean, when we opened, if we could have bought more land, we'd have bought it. Then we'd have had control and it wouldn't look so much like a second-rate Las Vegas around here.

"But we ran out of money. And then by the time we did have a little more money, everybody got wise to what was going on and we couldn't buy anything around the place at all."

Dick Says Take Care of 'Em

"Because I've had Dick Nunis on my tail and he says, 'You know, we've got to take care of these people.' He's got me workin' harder than I've ever worked before trying to enlarge the park to take care of the extra millions he thinks we're gonna gain every year.

"Now, he's got us working hard, honestly. I mean, he says: 'We gotta *expand* Fantasyland! We gotta *expand* other areas!' And he shows me this graph where you started here with three million, and the way he's got it, going up to ten million, and he may be right because this year we're just bulging at the seams here."

Roy Disney on the Ceiling

"You know my office is above my brother's, and I look down, when I see him walking on the ceiling. You know that's the time I go down and say, 'Let's put another ten million in Disneyland.' And lately he's been walking all around the ceiling."

Forty Millions Worth of Stuff

"But we do have plans to expand it, to open up new areas. It's like a sponge. You have to have these areas to absorb the people. And we hope to have these things going.

"You know of our plans for New Orleans and eventually the Haunted Mansion. We have a new Fantasyland coming; that'll be next year.

"And really, we've got about forty million dollars' worth of stuff planned for the next five years. Now, I don't know whether we've got the money to do it with, but...

"Thank God for *Mary Poppins* out there!"

Don't Rest on Your Laurels

"But at this time, ten years, I want to join my brother in thanks to all you people who've been here with us and have been a part of making this thing come across.

"I just want to leave you with this thought, that it's just been sort of a dress rehearsal and we're just getting started. So if any of you start to rest on your laurels, I mean, just forget it."

Next Year...Yeah!

"Well, I know...are you gonna have some dancing? These boys [the band] haven't done a damn thing all night.

"They've been sitting over there, on double time, no doubt, huh? And I think that was just a thanks and appreciation to my brother.

"To Joe Fowler, to all the boys, the top boys and all you people down the line who've been a part of this thing, as I say, we're just getting started.

The show goes on next year...yeah!"

The show *did* go on, the next day at 8 am, with some tired people who had enthusiastically joined the celebration.

And the *show* did go on the next year, with Walt personally opening "it's a small world", Primeval World, and New Orleans Square.

THIRTY-NINE

1966: The End of an Era

When Walt advised us not to "rest on our laurels", he wasn't kidding. And certainly he set the example of not resting on his laurels.

Although he was already absorbed with his new dream of EPCOT, a Utopian city in Florida, he was also proving that "Disneyland will never be completed as long as there is imagination left in the world."

Like others, I had the feeling that Walt Disney was immortal and not subject to the inevitability of death. As a result, when I heard through the grapevine that Walt was going into the hospital for surgery to correct an old injury from his polo-playing days, it seemed like a simple matter.

And the word from my network through Jack Olsen and Jack Sayers was that Walt came through in fine shape and was back at the studio giving his input on all of his new projects. So it was a total shock to learn that Walt was back in the hospital...with lung cancer. Even so, many of us believed that he would overcome this attack on his body.

The story is that Walt had ordered the plan-view drawings of EPCOT to be taped to the ceiling of his hospital room, and even as he was lying flat on his back, he made changes and came up with new ideas. I, for one, believe the story.

Eventually, we heard that he was dying. Jack Olsen had a good pipeline to the studio, and one day he told me the end could come at any time, but we wouldn't know until we heard it on the radio.

That same evening, after a couple of drinks at the Disneyland Hotel, I headed home to Laguna Beach. About halfway down Laguna Canyon Road, I heard on the radio that Walt had died.

The Disney family handled the matter quietly, without any Hollywood publicity. I didn't really accept the fact until the next day.

Walt died on December 15. What should we do about the next day?

Dick had to decide whether we should close the park or not. He called Lillian Disney, who felt that Walt would want "the show to go on".

We stayed open, but it was a sad day. Walt had a unique ability to reach out and touch people. He did this with everyone, regardless of status. He could charm kings, queens, presidents, and celebrities of all kinds. And at Disneyland, he was loved by food servers, maintenance people, sweepers, and everyone else in the cast. Although the park was open and operating the next day, many of us were openly and without embarrassment crying.

Some of us ended the day huddled together at the bar in the Disneyland Hotel...an informal wake. We all drank too much and expressed our grief in many different ways. People who no longer worked for Disneyland dropped by the hotel bar, and even some who had never worked there came in to join us in our loss.

And then there was the star, the one on the Matterhorn...

Three nights before this night, we had engineered and built a huge star which was placed by helicopter on top of the Matterhorn for the Christmas season. Now this was no ordinary star. It weighed 22 tons, and special equipment was needed to lift it to the peak of the Matterhorn. There was a highly complicated mechanism which was used for two years to make it turn...a great show.

Ted Crowell was director of Maintenance at that time, and making the star turn was a major, expensive problem for him. It was constantly breaking down. As the evening and the bar were both closing, Jack Sayers began to argue with Ted about the star which was supposed to turn. Ted tried to explain the problems, but Jack wouldn't listen.

As I made my way out of the bar, I heard Jack yell: "That star would be turning if Walt were alive!"

Jack was wrong, of course. Walt had given approval for the star *not* to be turning. And that may have been the first time I heard the phrase "if Walt were alive", but it certainly wouldn't be the last.

We at Disneyland were not the only ones who mourned Walt's death. The whole world joined with us.

On the first episode of *The Wonderful World of Color* after Walt died, no mention was made of his death. To this day some feel he is still alive.

It wasn't until four years later that Randy Bright included a segment on Walt's death in a training program. At the preview session of that program, an old studio hand became very upset. He couldn't accept that Walt was gone...even after all that time.

I've already mentioned my favorite of Walt's interviews—the one with the Canadian Broadcasting Corporation. The interview covers most of Walt's life, and Walt is in great form. Toward the end of the program, Fletcher Markle asks Walt what will happen to his Disneyland dream "after Disney", as he phrased it.

With a typical, thoughtful pause, Walt replied:

> Well, I think by this time, my staff, my young group of executives, and everyone else is convinced that Walt is right. That quality will win out.
>
> And so I think they're going to stay with that policy because it's proved that it's a good business policy. Give the people everything you can give them. Keep the place as clean as you can keep it. Keep it friendly, you know. Make it a real fun place to be.
>
> I think they're convinced and I think they'll carry on after, as you say, after Disney.

Walt had planned very well for Disneyland and the entire company, "after Disney".

Our sadness at Walt's death was not completely shared by the money men and stock brokers who didn't see any "collateral in dreams", as Walt had expressed it. Rather than dropping, the Disney stock immediately went up. Investors evidently felt that since Walt would no longer be around with his "dreams", Walt Disney Productions would be better off financially.

They also had confidence in Roy Disney's financial genius, although they didn't realize that Walt's brother was also dedicated to carrying out Walt's great dreams at Disneyland...and now at Walt Disney World in Florida.

As Walt had planned it, a top executive team headed up by Roy Disney, Card Walker, Donn Tatum, and Ron Miller immediately took over.

Plans for Disneyland and Walt Disney World were already solidly in place. We would live off them for many years.

The show would go on, the dream would survive. And I had one of my greatest challenges: to come up with an "After Disney" training program.

"Your Boss Was Here'

> Just after I returned to Disneyland, I had dinner at the Gourmet restaurant across the street at the Disneyland Hotel. I hadn't really noticed any familiar faces among the diners, but as I paid the check and got up to leave, my waitress said, "Your boss just left."
>
> I asked, "Who, Dick?" And she said, "No, dummy—Walt!"
>
> As I went out, I could see Walt and Lillian walking ahead of me, holding hands like two kids.
>
> There he was, world-famous, preparing to put on an important TV show, holding hands with his wife.

PART FIVE

The Show Goes On

1966–1970

FORTY

The Traditions of Walt Disney at Disneyland

Prior to Walt's death, we had been working on a new orientation program designed to re-motivate our cast after the tencennial hoopla.

All of our people identified with Walt Disney. You might even think everyone knew him personally. Our guests also identified with him. The question most frequently asked by our visiting guests was, "Is Walt Disney in the park today?"

Our new university theme would capitalize on this desire to identify with Walt. It was titled "YOU...Represent WALT DISNEY."

I'd had an idea which seemed good at the time. We ordered ten thousand little mirrors to be pasted in the new handbook to make the point that *you*, a cast member, were Walt's personal representative.

That crazy idea died along with Walt. And now, with the book nearly completed, we had to come up with a totally new approach, based on the reality of Walt's death.

Almost overnight, we had to switch from a theme based on Walt Disney walking the park, asking questions, changing attractions, raising hell with things that were wrong, to a park without him.

It was a bit like a family losing a loved and domineering father.

Fortunately, I had a dedicated and creative staff that included Gary Fravel, Randy Bright, Fred Kohler, Ralph Kent, Dawn Navarro, and Sara Mureno, all of whom would move on to better jobs.

Dick established the new program and handbook as top priorities, and we received help from everyone we asked, whether at the studio, at Disneyland, or at WED. We came up with the concept that Walt had left us with a set of TRADITIONS for which we were responsible if we were to keep his dream alive.

The basics in the handbook and program were similar to those we'd practiced for eleven years. They weren't new. To reinforce their legitimacy, we added a series of pictures of Walt and some of his quotes, which I still enjoy reading now, after these many years.

On How Disneyland Began

"Disneyland really began when my two daughters were very young. Saturday was Daddy's day. I would take them to the merry-go-round and sit on a bench eating peanuts. Sitting there alone, I felt there should be something built, some kind of family park where parents and children could have fun together."

On Disneyland's True Purpose

"I want Disneyland to be most of all a happy place—a place where adults and children can experience some of the wonders of life, of adventure, and feel better because of it."

On Integrity

"When guests come here, they're coming because of an integrity we've established over the years. They drive hundreds of miles. I feel a responsibility to the public."

On Hospitality

"The first year I leased out the parking concession, brought on the usual security guards—things like that. But I soon realized my mistake. I couldn't have outside help and still get over my idea of hospitality. Now we recruit and train every one of our people. I tell the security officers, for instance, that they are never to consider themselves cops. They are here to help people. The visitors are our guests."

On Doing Things Right

"Everybody thinks Disneyland is a gold mine—but we have our problems. We've got to work on them and know how to handle them. Trying to keep the park clean is a tremendous expense. And those sharp pencil guys tell you, "Walt, if we cut down on maintenance, we'd save a lot of money." But I don't believe that—it's like any other show on the road; it must be kept clean and fresh."

On Disneyland's Uniqueness

"Disneyland is not just another amusement park. It's unique, and I want it kept that way."

On Our Audience

"I don't like to kid myself about the intelligence and taste of audiences. They are made up of my neighbors, people I know and meet everyday. Folks I trade with, go to church with, vote with, compete in business with, help build and preserve a nation with. At Disneyland, the visitors are our guests. It's like running a fine restaurant. Once you get the policy going, it grows."

On Always Improving

"Whenever I go on a ride, I'm thinking of what's wrong with the thing and how it can be improved."

On Geniuses

"We have no geniuses at the studio. I have no use for people who throw their weight around, or for those who fawn over you because you are famous."

On Universal Appeal

"Part of the Disney success is our ability to create a believable world of dreams that appeal to all age groups. We try it in everything we do here, for the family. We don't actually make films for children. W make films that children can enjoy with their parents."

On Perfection

"I'm not the perfectionist anymore. It's my staff. They're the ones always insisting on doing something better and better. I'm the person trying to hurry them to finish before they spoil the job. You can overwork drawing or writing and lose spontaneity."

Our "After Walt" program was a success. Most of us wanted something to fill the void left by Walt, and the TRADITIONS were accepted.

That made it more important than ever for the university to create programs which would carry on the traditions, philosophies, and dreams that Walt left behind.

We now had a fine staff and good facilities and even a fairly good budget. We were recognized within the company and were increasingly getting notice in national magazines.

Things were not going quite as "smooth as whipped cream", but compared to the problems of the past, the situation was a happy one.

I should have know it wouldn't last.

FORTY-ONE

A Kick in the Teeth

*You may not realize it when it happens, but a kick in the
teeth may be the best thing in the world for you.*

— Walt Disney

Late in 1967, Dick got a call from Card Walker, the president of Walt Disney
Productions. Card asked Dick, Ted Crowell, and me to report to a meeting
in Roy Disney's conference room at 11 am.

We didn't have a clue as to what the meeting was about. Would it be
about some new training program? Were we to be recognized on our successful university programs?

No.

Card is a tall, dynamic, good-looking man who fit the role of a corporate
president. He is also a man of action, and without any preliminaries or happy
remarks, he said, "What we need is a training program for Disneyland."

Then he turned to usher into the room the man who would become the
new dean of the University of Disneyland. Card introduced Mike Vance.
Mike looked young; in his early thirties, I guessed.

After Mike left, Card suggested that we retain Mike on a consulting
basis to develop a training program. He asked the three of us what we
thought about the idea.

What was I supposed to say? "But Card, we have a program that is
working and is being copied by other theme parks and service industries
throughout the country"—?

Quite to the contrary, the only survivalist thing to do was to say it was
a good idea and then shake hands and get the hell out of there.

Dick, Ted, and I repaired to a local restaurant called the Carriage House
Inn. I ordered a drink before even looking at the menu. Then Dick, showing
his understanding and compassion, also ordered one, commenting, "I don't
ever drink at lunch. But in this case, I may have two or three."

Dick and Ted's empathy put some much-needed salve on my wounded
ego, and the drinks helped, too.

That evening I went home to my beachfront apartment to contemplate my future. The sound of the surf usually has a calming effect on me. That evening it helped, but not enough.

I approached my typewriter. I wrote a letter of resignation. It was followed by another, much stronger letter of resignation, full of the petulant ramblings of an adult who should know better.

I finally got the hurt out of my system.

The next morning I tore up the letters. Early in my work life, I learned not to quit a job without having another one lined up. When mad or frustrated, I've written dozens of letters saying "I quit!" The trick is to tear them up or burn them.

Calmer, I looked at life a little more realistically. I hadn't been fired. I still had Dick as a boss, although I'd be reporting in some ways to Mike.

I began to look on the bright side—and sure enough, that "kick in the teeth" turned out to be the best thing in the world for me.

FORTY-TWO

An Exciting New Career

As it turned out, the change was a great thing for Disneyland, the university, and particularly for *me*.

My style had been appropriate for the pioneering years, and it had been fun. But the cold reality is that I may be good at creating new programs, but I'm a lousy administrator. I get nervous and fidgety in meetings, and hate rules, regulations, policies, procedures, and—what were becoming popular—budgets.

Mike brought in a needed sophistication. The university was dressed up, and there was even an organization chart. He and I got along fine, and it was understood that I'd continue reporting to Dick. I even received a $25 per week raise.

With my new status, Dick approved of my going back to working on a part-time basis. This had many advantages for me, including an exciting stint as a consultant for a 97,000 acre development called Rancho California. Being part-time also gave me a feeling of security. A corporation is, after all, a business, and not a warm womb. At worst, I could only be half-fired.

Another advantage was that by not being tied down to day-to-day administration, I was available to perform any special assignments Dick would give me.

This gave me a chance to learn about the new happenings in Disneyland's future. It was the beginning of an exciting new career.

Dick was knee-deep in planning Disney World, and I was planning a vacation. Dick suggested that I mix business with my vacation and report to him on tourism in Florida. I jumped at the chance.

What is now the most popular recreation area in the world then consisted primarily of a tree farm which would supply the landscaping for the development.

Bill Evans invited me to visit the area and picked me up in his jeep. At the site I got out to walk around. Bill saw me and warned, "Look out for snakes!"

I didn't walk back to the jeep; I ran, and jumped in. Bill finished checking the trees, bushes, and grasses which would do well in Florida, and then we returned to the Gold Key Motel for a drink to settle my snake shakes.

I'd always wanted to drive down that many-bridged highway to the tip of the United States in Key West. I wanted to see the places where Harry Truman stayed and where Ernest Hemingway did his writing and drinking.

I also earned my pay by studying tourism in Florida which, at that time, didn't have much to offer. There was Busch Gardens and Cypress Gardens and *lots* of alligator farms.

Little did I know that Disney would change the entire pattern of tourism in the state. On that trip, however, my favorite attraction was Ernest Hemingway's old bar in Key West.

After Florida, Dick sent me up to Denver to develop a training program for our experimental venture called Celebrity Sports Center.

I don't know who talked Walt into building a family recreation center in Denver. Several celebrities, including Art Linkletter, were involved, but we ended up operating it. It was a great idea, with an Olympic-sized swimming pool, the largest bowling alley in the West, games for kids, a restaurant, merchandising, and a nursery for little children.

The center never made any money, and it was eventually sold.

On the other hand, it turned out to be a training center and proving ground for many future executives who would be key people in the future of Walt Disney World and other branches of the Disney organization. There were reasons for this:

- Managers were exposed to all phases of a facility: operations, food, merchandising, maintenance, finance, and promotion.
- The personnel manager, Jane Francis, acted as a den mother for young men, serving as a personal trainer.
- New managers could meet Walt Disney and other executives who were there to check it out...and possibly go skiing.

I always looked forward to any trip to Denver. There was a pioneering spirit about the place. As with the early days of Disneyland, there was a blending of people and talents.

The manager, Bob Allen, was a family man for a family center with a family feeling. Although I'd know Bob casually at Disneyland, we became life-long friends during my trips to Celebrity.

Adjacent to the Sports Center was a hotel and restaurant called the Cherry Creek Inn. It brings back memories of times when we could escape to that pleasant place to discuss training, the Disney organization, life, philosophy, raising children, and the world.

Bob was a 1955 pioneer who started as an Attractions host at a time when hours were frequently curtailed. He was always ready to work at anything, just to get the hours to pay his rent. Bob soon became a key supervisor for Dick, and then was selected by Tommy Walker to be a supervisor in Entertainment. By the time Celebrity had been purchased, Bob was well-known and highly respected. He was happy to take the job as Celebrity manager.

Although he called me his "guru", primarily because I was twenty years older, I think I learned more from him. He had an ideal family, and included me as sort of an extended family member.

While Disney World was in the planning stages, Dick picked Bob to head up the Florida operation. He managed to handle the work responsibilities, while at the same time remaining the kind of husband and father any wife or son would love to have.

He became vice president of Disney World and EPCOT Center where we'd continue to work together, and also philosophize about life. As it worked out, he was—if not an old "guru"—a wise counsellor who helped me out during my new "career" with Disney.

I remember a typical instance where Bob was a friend when I was in need.

The supervisors at Celebrity had an annual meeting where the plans for the year were discussed. It ended with a dinner, and then a traditional game of craps. Dick usually flew up for these meetings, but one year he couldn't make it, and I was his substitute. The year before, Dick had lost $200 with the dice, although he considers himself an expert. I had been warned about the sharpies up there, and I promised myself *not* to lose money. Unfortunately, I lost just as much money as Dick had lost.

At a farewell discussion at the Cherry Creek Inn, we bought a series of rounds of beer. Bob carefully kept the receipts for each order. He took me to the airport when I left, and as I prepared to board the plane, he handed me those receipts for the beer. "Van," he said, "I know you lost that money at the harmony session. Now if you'll put a little 'one' or 'two' in front of the totals on these receipts, maybe you can make up your losses. After all, it was for a good cause."

I followed his advice, but on the Disneyland expense accounts, you are required to list the names of people you entertained. I ran out of names. I was reading a Harold Robbins novel at the time, and so I used his name on my expense report: "Discussing training programs with Harold Robbins." Fortunately, Bob was the one to approve the expense report, and he was the only one who got a laugh out of my close relationship with the famous author.

Although Celebrity was small, I had become sort of a part-time training consultant. This relationship would lead to a major and challenging six months in my life.

FORTY-THREE

I Go Back to School

The folks at Celebrity Sports Center were a friendly group, even when they were taking my money shooting craps or bowling. One of the group was an outgoing, professional Irishman named Tom Murphy. He was the swimming coach at Denver University and a consultant to the Sports Center.

Tom gave me a tour of the Denver University campus, and the germ of an idea was planted in my middle-aged brain. I had promoted the notion of "lifelong learning". And now, could this apply to *me*?

My professional survival depended on my ability to understand the young generation of people who worked in our unique brand of entertainment and service. That same generation was confounding parents, educators, and people in the business world. This phenomenon was called the "Generation Gap". One premise of young people was, "You can't trust anyone over 30." And I was damned well over *that* age.

There was enough work for me to do here on a half-time basis, and Denver University seemed about the right-sized school for me. When I finally summoned up the courage to suggest to Dick that I go back to school for a semester while I worked at the Celebrity Sports Center, he agreed.

I found an apartment halfway between the center and the university, and was almost ready to face a new challenge. I doubt that I could have made it without Tom's help and guidance. In retrospect, I see that my fears were unfounded, but they were very real at the time.

I had been raised during the era in which many believed that "you can't teach an old dog new tricks". Would I be able to cope with the new tricks of the academic world?

After all, I was older than the *parents* of most of the students. Would people stare at me and wonder what I was doing there? Actually, I found that students were concerned about their own problems, and they accepted me as just another student—an *older* student, much older—but a student.

At the time, I wondered if it was smart to take out six months of my life to go back to school. In retrospect, it was the right move to make.

I found out that I could trust people *under* 30 and that they could trust me, if I respected them.

I took two courses in communications, which brought me up to date with the new trends of that era. And I received an "A" in both.

The folks at Celebrity were great friends, and I left with some sadness.

Heading back to Disneyland, I felt retreaded and ready for the excitement that was going to happen in Florida.

FORTY-FOUR

The Magic Kingdom Moves East

When I arrived back at Disneyland from my semi-sabbatical, the place was jumping. Disneyland itself was busier and more beautiful than ever. But there was a major difference now. The eyes, talents, and money of the Disney organization were now devoted to completing Walt's last great dream of Disney World and EPCOT. As a recent university student, my retreaded mind was now refurbished and ready to do something new. Florida would provide a challenge.

Somebody else will write the story of Walt Disney World, including EPCOT. In fact, it's a development which will provide action for several books. The creative purchase of the land and the innovative way the project was sold to the Florida legislature and to the city of Orlando is story enough for a full-length novel.

Although this book is about Disneyland, the so-called Florida Project was important for my survival...and fun. I'll pick at my memory and bring out some highlights of this new adventures.

"Invasion" may be a tough word, but that's what it was.

We Californians were going to establish a new theme park in a southern right-to-work state on the eastern seaboard. In addition to a small corps of executives who would be permanently transplanted, we would need to hire and train – very quickly – more people than made up the entire cast of Disneyland.

While WED was handling the "brick-and-mortar" aspects of building this miracle, Dick Nunis was planning for the people and operations factors, right down to the toilet paper supply needed for opening day.

By the time of the Florida invasion, Dick had been through a personal training program under Walt's direction. He had also been battle-trained at Disneyland, the Winter Olympics, and the New York World's Fair.

His planning profited from the mistakes made during the confusion of Disneyland's opening, and he added some new techniques which were eventually responsible for the success of this massive new venture.

A basic planning group for Walt Disney World had been formed under Bob Allen. Their offices were right behind the Market House on Main Street, and the music of an old-fashioned nickelodeon could be heard constantly during the day as they worked. Since I had no office, I moved in with this dynamic group.

Fred Brooks was a talented Disneylander who had both training and talent for attendance projections. His plans included the number of guests who would come to Walt Disney World on opening day, and in the months following.

Rich Battaglia worked with Fred, and concerned himself with things like work schedules. Both Fred and Rich would later be very successful in designing communities and them parks. Laraine Wright was the Dorothy Eno of the group. She was a brilliant, pert, charming young woman who kept everyone going. Laraine later moved to Florida and became the executive secretary of the Florida Executive Committee.

Meanwhile, Dick was carefully selecting his invasion force of 80 specialists who would go to Florida and remain there through the opening. Dick knew each one of these people personally, and they were familiar with his driving style of management. Our university now faced the added challenge of training an entirely new group of people.

You never said, "It's not my job," unless you wanted to be fired. "CAN DO!" was the operative response.

FORTY-FIVE

The University School of Resorts

We were the world's best when it came to running a theme park, but now for the first time we'd also be operating some large and sophisticated hotels. Dick's philosophy was the same as Walt's had been before Disneyland's opening. Rather than contracting the operations to professional managers, we'd run them the Disney way.

Once again he planned ahead, and made a lease agreement where we would operate what was called the Hilton Inn South with our own people. A young man, Dick Milano, was at the time manager of the University of Disneyland, and he had a degree from a hotel management school. Fortunately, he told us to "go with it", as we say in show biz.

My approach, with which Dick agreed, was generally based on our experience with new orientation back in the White House, fifteen years prior.

We might not know the details of running a hotel, but we knew about people, and properly trained and motivated people would be the answer. Most hotels at that time were operated by old-fashioned corporate bureaucrats. We would adapt only ideas from the progressive and successful ones. And our hotels would be *different*. The difference would be Disney.

Once again, we were armed with the best ammunition before we tackled this new challenge. Our handbook was titled *Hospitality IS the Hilton Inn South*. This was the first bible to be used for our hotels.

We always talk about "communications". But the service industries are loaded with a "language" which was and still is downgrading. Fortunately, we were able to come up with a new dialect of that language. We had proved that "host" and "hostess" had worked at Disneyland, and started with those terms, which included:

- *Lodging Hosts*. We don't have bell hops. First impressions are important. We have no bells, and nobody hops around here.

- *Reservation Hosts.* We don't have clerks. We have gracious hosts and hostesses who reflect our Disney brand of hospitality.
- *Food Hosts.* We don't have waitresses and bus boys. (I hate the term "boy" in any classification.)

By the time new people were screened, hired, and oriented, they knew that they were now part of the Disney Tradition, not just employees in a hotel. And, as word got around, we were able to select the best available people for our new concepts.

Fortunately, the operations director in charge of running the place was Bill Sullivan, a dedicated dynamo who had experience as manager of Adventureland in Disneyland.

Our hotel cast was enthusiastic, and they had a chance to meet nearly all of our top executives who came in at night to be served by, not bartenders, but Beverage Hosts. The main problem I had was with some graduates of a prestigious hotel management school. They hadn't learned that in the "Disney way" they were supposed to work *with* people, and help clean tables during rush period.

Today, our resorts are one of the largest and most sophisticated branches of the Disney Company. And we still practice some of the same principles we tried out in that small hotel in Orlando.

Before long, a training coordinator was selected to carry on the program, and I returned home to rest up for the final invasion of Florida.

FORTY-SIX

The Longest Ninety Days

Plans had been made, right down to the number of hot dogs which would be required on opening day. The first wave of the invasion force had moved permanently to Orlando under the direction of Bob Allen. The construction and design people were also there on a temporary basis.

And now, about 80 of us would be temporarily moved to Florida for the final pre-opening preparations. I don't recall the exact number of days. It was about three months, or maybe just *one* long day. I chose to stay at the Hilton Inn, where I felt "at home".

Although I had seen the Walt Disney World site several times before, when I arrived there about three months before opening, the place looked like a disaster area. Compared to Disneyland at the same point in its construction, or even Pleasure Island or Freedomland, this site was in terrible shape, and it was 80 times larger than Disneyland. I didn't know how it could possibly be ready to open on schedule. It looked *so bad* that I made a major financial mistake which I've lived to regret many times.

I often hear sad tales about how people would be rich if they had bought this or that, or not sold a lot in Beverly Hills. If you have ever had such a problem, I'll make you feel better.

I'd been making periodic trips to Florida, but when I saw the place 90 days before opening, I immediately remembered the financial debacles of Pleasure Island, Freedomland, and other losing theme parks.

Dick had been gracious in arranging for me to get some stock options. Now I'll admit I'm dumb when it comes to money things, but this time I outdid myself. I sold all my stock, and since then it has done nothing but go up and split and up some more and split again. When Dick heard what I'd done, he almost died laughing.

I wasn't the only one who could visualize a potential disaster. Roy Disney and the top executives had similar concerns. They had witnessed Dick's amazing capacity for leadership at Disneyland and the World's Fair, and had to be impressed with his plans for operating the park.

I don't know how it was arranged, but Dick was asked to take over the final construction of Disney World. He must have insisted on *total* authority, because he had it.

When the Nunis Mafia arrived in Orlando, Dick called a motivational meeting—Patton telling his troops they were going into a great battle and that they would win. Dick told us that we would have a successful opening, and then there would be a party we would never forget.

He fulfilled the promises in every way. We *did* open successfully, on time. And after opening he *did* throw a party at the Polynesian Resort which was huge and wet and *wild*!

John Edwards had been manager of the Celebrity Sports Center when I returned to school at Denver University. He and his family had made me feel at home in Colorado, and now that we were both staying at the Hilton Inn in Florida, we frequently joined each other for dinner.

One night Bill Sullivan dropped by and told us about the construction progress at the Contemporary Hotel. John said, "Why don't we move in there and become trial guests for training your staff?" Bill liked the idea, and so we moved in. Construction was still very much in progress, so our rooms had no air conditioning or other luxuries. But we pioneered the move, and soon others joined us. Bill opened a good bar at the hotel and arranged for some basic food. It was fun, and good training for the personnel.

The Disney organization was difficult for an outsider to understand. Our promotion-from-within policy resulted in close relationships. One person who penetrated the barrier was Howard Rowland, a New Yorker who had worked for U.S. Steel, and was in charge of constructing the Contemporary.

Once he remarked to me, "I can't understand this crazy organization." I explained that, especially here in Florida, it was "management by crony". Instead of saying, "That's crazy," he asked, "How do you become a crony?" I suggested that he start by taking Bill Sullivan to lunch.

That's what he did, and Howard went on to become a corporate vice president of Purchasing.During this long, three-month day, we were working under combat conditions. Dick was everywhere, motivating, pushing, getting the job done.

And he set the example by driving himself harder than he drove anyone else. I'm not sure how he does it, but I have a theory which I've developed from watching him in crisis situations. I think he has a forceful chat with his body, giving it these orders: "You are now going to be working for six months. You shall work seven long days a week. And you shall not catch a cold or anything else that will stop us."

It seems to work.

"Progress" in Orlando

On my first visit to Orlando, back when there was only a tree farm, the president of the Chamber of Commerce had given me a familiarization tour of the city. At the time, it was more advanced than Anaheim had been in 1955; and charming, as well. Most of the people I met there were enthused about the Disney invasion, but not everyone.

Winter Park was a quiet, artistic community similar to La Jolla in California. One of the key people in that community was quite direct about expressing his opinions. He felt we'd ruin the environment and "the place would be curb to curb with people".

There was a funky little airport, and one of the favorite local activities was to drive to a road near the airport and then park...just to watch the planes land and take off.

Fifteen years later, there would be a very modern airport, and the place *was* curb-to-curb people. I was constantly lost in the traffic.

Nobody has ever told me, nor have I ever read it, but it seems to me that Roy Disney promised that he would live long enough to open Walt Disney World.

Although Walt left his dream in solid executive hands, it was Roy's financial genius that made it possible to open the new park with very little debt. And I was fortunate to have a memorable dinner with this very human man.

I was staying at the Hilton Hotel and went down for dinner on a Sunday. At that time, Orlando had a "No Alcohol on Sunday" blue law. Roy came in with Joe Fowler. He stopped to talk to some Disney executives who were there with their wives, then he and Joe came over to my table.

"Put your book down, Van, we're going to join you," he said. And they did. We had a delightful dinner, with Roy telling me about the progress at the California Institute for the Arts, which the Disney family financed. When the check came Roy reached for it, but I said, "Roy, it would look good on my expense report if I took *you* to dinner."

He immediately agreed. "Sure, Van, it all comes out of the same pot."

Meanwhile, Dick was fighting for the nearly $400,000 it would cost for his latest idea. A research team had found a way to create waves which would build up across the lagoon facing the Polynesian Hotel. Surfers could ride in on their boards to entertain he guests, and children and body surfers would enjoy an inland ocean experience. Most executives felt it was impractical, but Dick kept trying to sell Roy on the idea.

At a Club 55 meeting, Roy and Dorothy Eno were discussing Dick's wave machine when Roy winked at Dorothy and said, "That young whippersnapper will get his wave machine."

Note: Dick never gives up. In 1989, seventeen years later, there was a beach and a working wave machine, and Dick—then the president of Walt Disney Attractions—expertly surfed on the first wave at opening.

Dick well remembered the "Black Sunday" of Disneyland's opening. We weren't ready for the guests. At Walt Disney World, he decided not to have a huge press party on opening day. And before opening, using many of us as trial guests, we operated the park as if it were open—working rehearsals. As a result, on opening day, the cast was relatively well-trained for the first paying guests in the Magic Kingdom.

Opening day for any theme park is exciting...and suspenseful, as well.

Fred Brooks had spent years planning for the number of guests who would appear on opening day. His projections were used to determine how much food and merchandise would be needed. Now we would find out how accurate his predictions were. Unfortunately, Dick's slow opening had slowed down the crowds.

Fred was about 20,000 off, and he was in such shock that he was sick for several days. I think that Dick was happy, perhaps thinking of something Walt had said: "These people came here and had a good time. They didn't have to stand in line. They'll leave and tell all their friends."

When I arrived at the Orlando International Airport for the trip home, the waiting area was filled with veterans of the Florida invasion. "Haggard" was the word for the way most of us looked. One of the group was Len Jones, our safety engineer, and fortunately he didn't drink.

When the flight attendant passed out those little bottles of liquor, Len passed his along to me. As a result, I was in fine condition when my fiancée, Stel Webb, met me at the airport back home.

It seemed like a good idea to spend the weekend at the Century Plaza Hotel, and I put it on my expense account. Later, Laraine Wright slipped the expense report onto Dick's desk in Florida, after first making sure he was in a good mood. His sharp eye caught the hotel bill, but Laraine told me that he said, "What the hell, he did a good job," and signed the report.

And now I was back "home", at Disneyland.

PART SIX

Back Inside the Berm

1970–1979

FORTY-SEVEN

The Seventies

I was back "home".

Walt Disney World and EPCOT Center may be bigger and many times more complex, but my heart belongs to Disneyland. The last time I went to Disney World, I actually was lost once or twice. I like the intimacy, the history, and the memories of Disneyland.

I was also back "inside the berm". I'll confess I'd never heard of the term until the designers kept mentioning it. The dictionary defines a berm as a "ledge or space between ditches of a fortification". In Walt's Midwest, berms were elevated earthen mounds used to prevent flooding.

Walt would go to any expense to prevent "visual intrusion" into the stage for his show. When the State of California raised the level of the Santa Ana Freeway, he paid to raise the height of the berm. When he saw telephone wires while taking a trip on the *Mark Twain*, he paid to have the objectionable wires placed underground.

But now, while the publicity and attention of our executives was directed toward Walt Disney World, some problems typical of the "outside world" began creeping into our spectacular show.

The story goes that Walt was giving Billy Graham a tour of the park. The evangelist commented about how different Disneyland was from the real world. Walt responded emphatically, "No! *This* is the real world as it should be. It is well-planned for the enjoyment of people. It is clean, safe, and a place for families. It's a friendly place where people can enjoy their lives."

Walt was right, of course, If the real world is as it's depicted on the nightly news, then we really don't know the difference between reality and fantasy. If it is a world of constant wars, gangs, rapes, child abuse, homeless people, pollution of the very air we breathe and the water we drink, then it might better be called the "insane world".

For years we vigorously fought any "visual intrusion", but the area bounding our parking lot had been invaded by high-rise hotels, including the Disneyland Hotel. We have the Santa Ana Freeway to thank for the fact that there can be no development on the area that can be seen from inside the park. Of course, there was not much we could do when Harbor Boulevard became a haven for hookers.

But inside the berm, things were happening—both good and bad—in what Walt would call the real world.

The Cinderella Years

I reflected the feelings of many people when I would complain to Dick that we were the Cinderella in the company family.

And it was sort of true. This new sister in the east had taken many of our key people. All profit was poured into the Florida bank account. They had even appropriated our name—Magic Kingdom—and borrowed our Main Street vehicles, which were not returned for years. We were promised some "hand-me-downs" Florida, which we did receive, eventually.

Working the Graveyard Shift

Some executives try to make the midnight to 8 am shift sound more attractive by calling it the "third shift". Forget it. It is the "graveyard shift".

During one critical union negotiation, Dick had worked around-the-clock selling the company's proposal. When he met with the men on graveyard, he received a lot of flack. And he realized that they had some legitimate complaints.

He asked me when I'd like to start working the graveyard shift for a while. I knew the answer and replied, "Tomorrow." He said I'd picked the right date.

I worked graveyard for a month. At the end of each night, I'd type up a report of the problems I'd encountered and my recommendations for solving them. Based on those reports, Dick and Ron Dominguez made some positive changes.

There is a feeling of camaraderie among those who work that shift, and I made some friendships which have endured for years. Al Grills and Roger Banner remained friends, even after some tough days which will be mentioned later in this story.

Although my period on the graveyard shift was short, I found out how easy it was to hate one's friends working the day shift. In the morning, just as I would be leaving after a night in the park, in would drive my managerial colleagues, fresh, neatly dressed, and ready for a normal day's work, while I would be heading home to *try* to get some sleep.

Veepograms

Fortunately, I was forced to take a typing course in high school. It has led to the basic form of communications I've always used with Dick.

Dorothy Eno came up with the name. If I was *mad* about something, I'd go home and write a note, on yellow paper, venting my frustration. Rather than ignoring these "veepograms", Dick encouraged them. He might disagree, but he'd read them.

A Hotel Deal Falls Through

Because of its name, people have always thought that we owned the Disneyland Hotel. We've been blamed for any problems that have happened there.

The fact is that it was owned by the Wrather Corporation, which paid us to use the Disneyland name. Jack Wrather was a personal friend of Walt Disney's. He had been the only person who was willing to gamble his money on building a class hotel near the new theme park. In 1974, Wrather seemed willing to sell, and we had enough money—represented by stock—to buy the hotel.

Dick assigned a dynamic executive, Jim Cora, to plan for the future management of this new property, and he included me on his dedicated team. Unfortunately, our Disney stock took a major tumble, and the deal fell through. We held a sad wake, Jim and his team were to move ahead to play a greater part in Disneyland history.

Reorganization!

The term "reorganization" strikes terror in the hearts of the bravest people in any organization. At Disneyland, it causes panic.

Corporations, including Disneyland, are a bit like people who go on diets. They accumulate a little fat, and suddenly they discover that they are critically overweight. At Disneyland, the fat is revealed not by stepping on scales or being warned by a doctor, but when a finance person looks at the Profit and Loss Statement.

Walt Disney's "Uncle Walt" image never prevented him from keeping the organization alive by cutting back, as you've seen during the early days.

Perhaps one reason I was involved in this reorganization was that I had been around in 1955 when Walt created a plan that we call Area Management, with a key person responsible for each "geographic" area within the park, like Tomorrowland.

It was the first major restructuring since the end of the Sayers Era. It is impossible to be totally objective when jobs and careers are at stake. There were terminations and tears, both by some who were leaving (many to get better jobs) and by those of us who stayed and lost good friends.

Where's the Key?

Dick's son, Rich, was one of those attending a Grad Night for his Laguna Beach school. Dick was there, walking the park, when Space Mountain broke down. He immediately headed there to check out the problem.

The problem, it turned out, was the need for a small replacement part which was locked in a cabinet. "Where's the key?" he asked. It seems that the only key was held by a Maintenance person who could not be located.

It *was* incomprehensible. When Dick's adrenaline starts to flow, it is time to take cover. He literally picked up the huge cabinet, bashed it against the wall, and broke it open.

"There," he said, "is your damned spare part." Then he strode back into the park to raise hell about anything else he could find wrong.

The Left-Handed Skillet Initiation

Foods cast members have ingenious ways of getting the most possible fun out of their work assignments. One way is to initiate new hosts and hostesses by sending them all over the park searching for "specialized" equipment.

On one occasion, a rookie host assigned to the New Orleans Main Kitchen was directed by the cook to "go to the Plaza Inn and borrow a left-handed skillet".

The Plaza Inn folks were in on the joke, and they quite solemnly informed the rookie that they didn't loan out their left-handed skillet, as it was too difficult to replace. They sent the host to the Case de Fritos (now called Casa Mexicana) where the cast members who were also privy to the entire set-up gave him the desired skillet.

But alas, when he finally returned to the New Orleans Main Kitchen, he was told that the skillet was too small, and so off he went on another "wild skillet chase".

A Record Year

After years of sending manpower, money, and machines to Florida, the park finally received a major attraction in return: Space Mountain. Even after the research and development that Walt Disney World had invested, Space Mountain was an architectural and technological challenge for us.

A 20-foot foundation was dug in Tomorrowland so that Space Mountain would not overshadow our castle, which is much smaller than the one at Disney World.

A new attraction always gives us a chance for a lot of promotional hoopla, and Space Mountain was a cause for celebration in a big way. For the first time in our history, our annual attendance went over 10 million guests. And among our important guests were the real-life *Mercury* astronauts. The excitement helped build back morale after the deal for the Disneyland Hotel had fallen through, and the painful reorganization.

And for me: I found a new office and some new excitement.

During the hotel negotiations. I'd worked in a fancy office in the hotel's executive wing, but now, for about the 13th time, I was once again without a place to hang my occupational hat.

Fortunately, Jim Cora took me on as his training consultant, and fixed me up with an office used by Monsanto before we took over the Adventure Through Inner Space attraction. Jim is a true believer in training, and together we worked on some interesting leadership studies.

In recounting these flashbacks from what I now think of as Disneyland's Cinderella years, I missed one major crisis which happened at the very beginning of the decade.

It was Yippie Day at Disneyland.

FORTY-EIGHT

Yippie Day at Disneyland

We have an entire department paid to attract special parties and conventions to Disneyland. One event we did *not* seek out was the national convention of Yippies on August 7, 1970.

It turned out to be a major historical event for Disneyland, for Anaheim and neighboring cities, and for the nation, and it marked the beginning of the end for the Yippies themselves. It deserves a bit of background.

For those who were not around at the time, an essay in *U.S. News and World Report* described the late sixties and early seventies in this way:

> Yes, Virginia, things were not always as they are today. There was a time before you and your playmates were born when American was a panorama of tumult, the time of the 60s radicals. They marched, they sat in, they trashed college offices, they burned draft cards, they poured blood on Selective Service records. Vietnam was part, but not all of their cry. They were sincerely bent on remaking the world.

And Disneyland was to become a staging area for the most radical branch of the youth movement.

The year 1970 was about the peak of activity for the Hippies who felt alienated from society and who showed their resentment through riots, picketing, and anti-war demonstrations. Yippies were the most radical faction of the general Hippie movement. Their name came from the *Youth International Party*. They tried every means of getting publicity through TV or print coverage.

The Yippies had received international publicity when they invaded the Democratic Convention in Chicago in 1968. The Chicago demonstration was a huge success from the standpoint of showing riots, people being jailed, a pig being nominated for president, and a general attack on American values. The leaders felt that Disneyland would be an even better stage for publicity, so they decided to "breach our berm and attack our castle".

The invasion was billed as National Yippie Day, and they had several special events planned:

- A Black Panther breakfast at Aunt Jemima's Pancake House.
- Snake dances throughout the park.
- The liberation of Minnie Mouse (no one seems to know exactly what that was to entail).
- The capture of Tom Sawyer Island, making it the national headquarters for the Yippies.

The organizers didn't expect the counter-offensive personally directed by Dick. His counter-offensive included:

- The city of Anaheim and the police department (including a SWAT team) were on alert and assigned to our property.
- A force of 150 police from neighboring cities in Orange County was on hand to assist, if necessary.
- Our own Security hosts had been given special training for the anticipated event.
- Those of us who wouldn't be much good in a fight were dressed as tourists to walk the park and report any incidents.

Everyone who was around on that day has his or her personal experiences—almost like opening day. I can only give you a picture of the day through my own eyes.

The park opened at 8 am. We were ready.

Dick, Card Walker, and Roy Disney were stationed at the Main Entrance. With great moderation, they talked to the Yippie leaders. "Have your fun, but don't disrupt!" they said.

It would be a 30,000 attendance day. The Yippies had planned on 3,000 people of their own, but only about 300 showed up.

My job was to walk the park dressed as a tourist and report any unusual incidents. Evidently, my disguise was not too good. As I strolled around Tom Sawyer Island, Yippies yelled, "Hark, hark, a narc!"

There were a few minor incidents, such as snake dances and small demonstrations. But the day was smoother than anticipated, until about five in the afternoon.

The day was winding down toward the time of our retreat ceremony, during which the American flag is ritually lowered. As yet, the Yippies hadn't caused the riot they had planned. They congregated on Main Street, and soon began to harass other guests. Like a general in charge of defense, Dick had kept his cool—an example of grace under pressure.

But when one of the Yippie leaders began to raise a Viet Cong flag with a red star and marijuana leaf, they had gone too far. And the harassment of guests had become impossible to tolerate any longer.

Finally, with his adrenaline flowing, Dick picked out one of the most obnoxious leaders, charged him, and physically carried and dragged him out of the park. At that point, the police moved in. Rather than picking out the 300, we closed the park. All guests were given re-entry tickets, and, as planned, we apologized for the closing.

Of the 300 Yippies, 23 were arrested. Their grand statement had backfired.

I found it interesting that our world audience thought of Disneyland as *their* dream and resented the Yippie intrusion. Thousands of letters flowed in from across the country, congratulating us for preserving *their* Disneyland. The media coverage was uniformly favorable in reporting the way we handled the situation.

Most of the Hippies and Yippies have now grown up and are now part of the Establishment. Their organization died, and Disneyland kept right on growing.

These 76 million Baby Boomers had their problems, but nothing compared to mine: I was almost 65 damned years old!

....

Hair

Is there one policy problem which has been around since our pre-opening orientation until today, and perhaps tomorrow? Yes, and crazy though it may seem, it is hair!

Hair had been a problem in 1955. But it was the outlandish styles of that era for women. I helped establish the policy for not hiring women with huge beehives or hair tinted green or blue.

In those early days, we might worry about tattoos, but most young men came in with neat, short haircuts. That changed in the 1960s.

The hairy revolution of that decade (and the decades following) was in direct contradiction to the "Disneyland Look": a natural boy-and-girl-next-door appearance for which we had become famous. Unfortunately, our young men and women were no longer buying our 1955 concept. Neat hair cuts were called "side walls". It was rumored that only three groups had the neat look—Marines, narcotics agents, and men working at Disneyland.

Some men turned down our jobs because of our grooming policy. And, as soon as a man quit, the first thing he'd do was to grow a moustache or beard

Dick asked me to write a manual covering all company policies, from A to Z. But I disagreed with the hard line on grooming, and I told Dick I'd have trouble writing that policy.

"OK," he said, "then you just leave "G" out of your alphabet, and I'll do that one."

Eventually, the hair styles changed, and the problem was not as acute. But in the early 1980s, young people found another way to drive parents and teachers crazy, with the "punk look".

FORTY-NINE

Along Came Sixty Five!

Attention all friends, colleagues, and particularly editors!

Fess up now. When you saw the title of "Sixty Five" you thought I'd lost track of my story and was going to repeat 1965 and our Tencennial Celebration. Nothing like *that*. I, your faithful pioneer, was about to become sixty-five years of age. I was supposed to *retire*, with some of this story yet to come.

The truth is that I'd been too busy and having too much fun to think about retirement. As a result, when Lucky Smeltzer, the den mother for retirees, called to say I had to sign up for Medicare and Social Security, it was a shock.

Retire? Hell, no! I didn't believe in it then, and as I write this at age 77, I still don't. But that doesn't mean that the mandatory law back then agreed with me.

Survival. After all, I'd survived many changes in bosses, work assignments, office locations, and organizations. The challenge now was to find a way to cope with being born in 1912 and the policy that required me to go find myself a golf cart.

I told myself that I could write handbooks, so why not start a campaign for my own survival where my roots were firmly planted?

I did my research and found out that there were more myths than facts about aging. At that time, President Reagan had not been elected, and then re-elected, as our eldest president at 76.

I wrote a book titled *Career Planning for Senior Adults*. This led to a newspaper story, "Hot Stuff on the Labor Market". I used the sales point that Walt Disney was going strong at age 65, and that Roy Disney headed up Walt Disney World in his 70s.

I pointed out that some older employees worked harder than younger ones, and used Walt's quote to help prove my point: "I've got a lot of guys around here [the studio] who have retired, but they haven't told me about it yet." I suggested that the company would save money by *not* giving me a retirement party, a corporate event which I hate with a passion.

I bombarded Dick with my campaign. I worked harder than I'd ever worked seeking a job. It paid off.

When I reached my Medicare qualification day, Dick presented me with a contract to sign. It would let me stay on with the company part-time. He also quietly slipped me the posters and plaques I might have received at some party. I could have hugged him, but he doesn't care much for such things.

As it turned out, my age became an asset for an exciting era in my life.

FIFTY

Happiness Goes to Tokyo

Jim Cora and I were having coffee when he told me that he'd been offered a job as head of Operations for our first-ever Disneyland in a foreign country.

Fortunately, we had worked together on training at Disneyland, Walt Disney World, and the hotel deal. He planned to take the challenge, and offered me the task of working with the orientation training team.

Some of us at Disneyland were not enthused about this new Disneyland in Japan. After all, Walt had said there would be only *one* Disneyland.

But, of course, plans moved forward, and the university established our first international training program—and it was extensive. About 120 executives and trainees from the Oriental Land Company came to Disneyland, WED, MAPO, the Disney Studio, and Walt Disney World. They observed, kept diaries, and actually worked on the jobs they would supervise in Tokyo. And eventually they became friends with their counterparts in the Disney organization. I hate to confess it, but they may know more about Disneyland than *we* do.

While working on the training program, I started checking into Japanese literature, history, and culture, but Dick straightened me out on that.

The president of the Oriental Land Company had told him, "Don't Japanese it up!" They wanted it to be pure Disneyland and pure American. Even so, I read *Shogun* and other books about Japan, and I developed a great respect for the Japanese culture.

Dick and Jim planned their invasion as carefully as General MacArthur had done 40 years earlier. We need handbooks, an orientation training plan, and visual aids which would show that we were the super-professionals. Jim formed a team of bright, young men and women with whom I'd work and from whom I'd learn. The planning was similar to what Dick and I had done back in 1955. The difference was that now we had the best of equipment and a staff of brilliant young people.

I had survived that dreaded age of 65. And now, thanks to Tokyo, I was to find that age and youth could be merged to advantage.

Heading up our dynamic group was "Bubba" Allen, the son of Bob Allen, and a pen pal when he was in college. He had put the team together and included me to write the handbook, in both English and Japanese. I thought my role was to give input and let the young folks produce it in Tokyo. But in a planning meeting, Dick asked if I had my passport. "Why me," I asked. "Because," Dick answered, "you are going. The average age of the top executives of the Oriental Land Company is 67, and you'll be our "ancient one".

The group gave me a name tag with the title "O.F. Number One", standing for, as we understood it, "Old Fart"—or "Old Friend", if one prefers.

Finally, we were ready to head overseas. Our happiness package included an amazing visual presentation, plus handbooks and cards.

Bob Allen and Steve Kasper had preceded us to plan the presentation, and Dick, Jim Cora, Jim Passila, and I followed them for the introduction of the training for Tokyo Disneyland. We'd be making this first presentation to all the top executives involved in the new park.

The room was set up in rather sterile-looking quarters in a Mitsui office building. The Japanese executives were seated according to status, with the most senior men in the center front seats. We had been warned that they might be stone-faced, but they would listen. I was glad to receive the warning.

Dick and I teamed up to give the pitch-card presentation. He was the leader and preceded me with historical and motivational information. Dick was already a pro when it came to working through an interpreter. His physical presence is so strong that people believe him even if they can't understand what he says. I followed with my presentation of the essential way of serving guests in a Disneyland show.

Although the Japanese executives would never know it, the presentation was very nearly the same as the one we had given in that old White House, during pre-opening days.

On our last night in Tokyo, we attended a reception in a beautiful Mitsui mansion. It was friendly, but formal. Speeches were given. A key Japanese executive spoke about the need to control and cut costs. Dick, trained by Walt Disney, would not sacrifice quality on the basis of expense. When he rose to respond, he asked Harry, the interpreter, to quote him *exactly*.

Very distinctly, using every pause, he pointed out to all the Japanese executives that *our tradition* was one of quality regardless of cost.

There was a silence. His statement was made with a very positive smile. In football terms, he might have thought of it as a "key block", a blow against the finance people who want to sacrifice quality for costs. I'm sure that his message, in those lovely surroundings, made an impression which would survive long past Tokyo Disneyland's opening in 1983.

The Tokyo trip had been my shortest experience with a new project, but it was a memorable one.

I had learned to like the Japanese people, their culture, their history. I envied those who were staying on. But it was time for me to go.

The day before we left, Dick, Jim, and I were given a tour of the Tokyo Disneyland "site" and the community in which it would be located. There was a sign, on undeveloped land, stating that *this* would be the location of the castle. Here I could see what had at one time been "the sites" at Anaheim; Orlando; and Wakefield, Massachusetts. I just couldn't visualize this great new Disneyland in a foreign country.

The night before we left, Dick and Jim took Bubba, Steve, and me out to a farewell "thank you" dinner. And then it was back to Disneyland and some unhappy times in the "Happiest Place on Earth".

PART SEVEN

Mid-Life Crisis

1979–1987

FIFTY-ONE

Happiness Takes a Beating

In 1980 we celebrated our 25th anniversary. It was a BIG YEAR.

We went all out in every possible way. There was a special parade, an all-night party, and tremendous hoopla, including the release of 25,000 silver, white, and blue balloons. My friends helped me produce a memorable evening for the Club 55 pioneers. The media descended on us, and I became one of the old-timers who were searched out for interviews.

We reached our peak attendance of 11.5 million guests. Although I had complained about Disneyland being the neglected Cinderella in the corporate family, in 1980 *we* were on stage—that special first child.

But after the celebration was over, we had some of the most depressing periods in my Disneyland experience.

Who knows about the life span of a dream? I certainly don't. We were, however, 25 years old. We had been through childhood and the teen years. And now, it seemed to me, we had a mid-life crisis. We survived, and changed, but we had some rough bumps.

Sometimes when one thing goes wrong the so-called "domino effect" occurs, and then other problems are created.

One key domino at Disneyland has always been the attendance. If it drops, even slightly, panic arises. And after our 25th anniversary year, attendance began to fall.

We then went through a period that was characterized by attacks, from within by two major union strikes, and from without by a corporate raid on our company. Not to mention:

- After the longest run in TV history, our Disney Sunday night program was cancelled. Whenever Disneyland was featured on the show, it has been an interesting, hour-long commercial for us. No more.

- We were no longer the "only game in town". We had competition from shopping malls, cable TV, home movies, and other local and national attractions.

- We'd always prevented people from the same sex dancing together, but two men brought a suit against us and won.
- A young man was stabbed during a fight at a special dance in Tomorrowland, and the press blamed us.
- Because of low attendance, it was necessary to cut hours and lay off people, and that is always a guaranteed way to create discontent.

As a special added morale dampener, two of our long-time top executives retired. We already had enough problems, but now we had to go through the first change in our upper-level management since Walt's death.

Our "after Walt" top executive team had been solidly in place for nearly 15 years. As chairman and president, respectively, Donn Tatum and Card Walker had carried on Walt's traditions. They had kept the "family feeling", and we had become accustomed to their style of management.

Now the grapevine became active with rumors of who would be the next two top executives. I'm prejudiced, of course, and thought that Dick might become president.

But it was finally announced that Ray Watson, an Orange County land developer who had been active on the Board of Directors would be chairman, with Ron Miller, Walt's son-in-law, as president.

Internal problems and management changes exist in all industries, but when people are producing a dream, and creating happiness as its by-product, it is a different situation.

Over the next few years, the public was to learn that the "Happiest Place on Earth" had a few problems of its own.

Perhaps this chain of bad events started with a strike of our Maintenance unions.

FIFTY-TWO

My "Cronies" Walk Out

For the first time in park history, we had a major strike. In this case, it involved all of our skilled craftsmen. It was particularly heartbreaking for me, as I had some good friends in the union—Dick called them my "cronies".

As a member of management, I'd have to drive into the park right past my friends who were carrying picket signs. Since I'd seen how hard these friends worked, I leaned toward their point of view. To make things worse, it was a time of double-digit inflation.

Management contended that our rates were already better than those paid for comparable jobs at places like Knotts Berry Farm. Union members countered that our quality of maintenance, and thus their level of effort, could not be compared with what went on at other parks.

As so often happens, the hardliners in management and the hardliners in the unions got their way, and my friends "hit the bricks" (or asphalt).

When it came to the strike organization, management completely outclassed the unions. Each union had its own leaders, and they didn't coordinate their activities well. They were up against a single force headed by canny management, with additional backing from the Disney Studio and Walt Disney World.

Since most of our supervisors had been promoted from within the company, we had a corps of people who could handle basic maintenance work. In addition, we were able to fly in a special task force of experienced people from Disney World.

My striking friends and I continued to talk to each other, but as in a major marital dispute, the relations were not the same. One of the pleasant things about working with Maintenance was the "schmoozing"— swapping jokes and gripes and gossip. I could always count on some new joke over coffee. During and after the strike, this source of fun dried up, but only for a while.

The maxim is that nobody wins in a strike, and in this case it was definitely true. The union members lost earnings and gained nothing. The company also lost, since the pride and dedication of many of its people had been seriously wounded.

A strike—and this would not be the last one—just does not fit in with my philosophy. It is difficult to "create happiness for others" when those who produce it are unhappy and distrustful.

Unfortunately, two years later we would encounter another labor crisis which would receive national attention.

FIFTY-THREE

"The Friendliest Picket Line"

One newspaper billed it as a "friendly picket line". There is no such thing as a friendly picket line, or a friendly strike. It was a tragic strike.

Our original union contract was a shotgun marriage with 29 unions. There were two major groups covered by the contract. One included the Maintenance crafts—mechanics, carpenters, painters, and others who worked backstage. The other group was made up of our "service unions", including cast in Attractions, Merchandising, Custodial, and the warehouse.

During the unfortunate Maintenance strike, the service people had continued to walk right past the pickets, which did not promote a feeling of teamwork. One of my Maintenance friends put it this way: "I just hope those people strike sometime, so I can walk right past *their* pickets."

For months, the negotiations dragged on. As before, the hardliners on both sides talked louder than the moderates. Finally, the unions went out, and once again I had to drive to the park past friends I'd known for years.

The union members lost money, as well as the reason for the strike. The company lost valuable time that could have been spent dealing with other problems, and it got negative publicity around the world for its handling of the situation. But for me, it was a tragedy which went contrary to everything I'd been preaching for years.

My sympathies were with the unions, and I expressed them regularly to Dick. Any other executive would have fired me, but he listened—although he disagreed.

For a few reasons, the union had picked a bad time for a major strike. There was a national anti-union sentiment, with companies negotiating for "take backs" of rates and benefits. We'd expected an attendance bonanza from the 1984 Summer Olympics, but people stayed away in droves.

There were a few bad incidents, but overall it *was* the friendliest and most innovative picket group. They could not, however, bring Walt back to settle the strike, and they forgot that Walt had been the toughest hold-out when unions organized the studio, long before Disneyland.

Although I found that my relations were strained with people who had been my friends for years, it was worse for others. There were husbands and wives on opposite sides of the strike. A supervisor might have to walk right past his or her spouse who was walking the picket line. Fathers, sons, mothers, daughters, brothers, sisters might be on opposing sides. And even *within* the unions there were pro-strike and anti-strike factions.

It all boiled down to a basic money problem. Company profits were down, due in part to high wages and generous benefits. At the same time, long-service personnel were losing real earnings due to inflation and, in particular, soaring rents in the area.

Disneyland was not like an industrial plant that could be closed down. Despite some rough spots, the park was operating with managers and supervisors taking over for the striking hourly workers.

I ended up taking passports at the Main Gate. I was really at my best on Thursdays and Fridays, when senior citizens flock to the park because they get a discount. Since anyone can tell that I'm old, I got a kick out of asking every female guest with the slightest glint in her eye for age identification. They knew I was kidding, but they just loved to have someone ask for proof of their "senior" status. They left my turnstile giggling happily. I *was* creating happiness!

Very few people stayed away from Disneyland because of the pickets. On the other hand, it was sickening to see the strikers on TV and to read about the dispute in the daily papers. A federal mediator had been called in, but even she couldn't find a proper compromise.

Without question, the bad publicity was hurting the magic of Disneyland. Although the company could continue to operate—and so, in that sense, the strike had failed—this was not our type of positive public relations. At the same time, the unions were out on a limb, and they needed some face-saving way to climb back.

Although others were involved, it was Dick Nunis who ended the strike.

I was working on an "after strike" healing plan at the time, and so I don't know all the details, but Dick came up with a compromise that both management and the unions could accept. Everyone was happy that the nightmare– this mid-life crisis—had been resolved.

Dick had been as saddened about the strike as I had been, though his responsibilities were quite different. He knew that our people were Disneyland people...who happened to be union members. He knew that they have pride, are dedicated, and need respect.

As one union employee said, "I may disagree with Dick, but we respect him and we *trust* him."

Unfortunately, our "mid-life crisis" was not to end with the strike settlement.

FIFTY-FOUR

From Main Street To Wall Street

Although the strike was a major crisis, it was mild compared to what was to be the greatest change in Disney history.

I had read about companies being bought and sold by other companies, and financiers practicing "greenmail" (as opposed to blackmail). I'd heard about "friendly takeovers" and "hostile" takeovers and "white knights" and "black knights"...things like that. But that stuff happened to *other* companies, not Disney.

Now, however, the fate of Disney was big news, and we'd hear about people and companies who were competing to buy out Walt Disney Productions and, of course, Disneyland.

Disneyland's Main Street was being manipulated by the money men of Wall Street.

The story of these high-level manipulations is well told in the book Storming the Magic Kingdom by John Taylor. But what was the future for those of us who had never known anything but the friendly control of Walt Disney's family and designated executives?

In any presentation I've given at any company, I've never been dumb enough to say, "We're just one big happy *family*." After all, more people are killed in family fights than at the workplace.

But I *have* referred to our "Disneyland Community", and I've worked on the concept of a "corporate village", where we worked together to survive in a cold, cruel world. And when we talked about the "Disney Democracy", it was rather true. Obviously, it wasn't all ideal. We had our strikes and our politics, but it was the best company I'd ever worked for.

And now we were to become pawns in a battle for profit.

The wheelers and dealers in these takeover battles sit in offices and have meetings. But at Disneyland, we guaranteed a "fresh show every day", and said it was the "Happiest Place on Earth". And we had to do this while a series of rumors which affected us all made the rounds daily.

The grapevine was overworked, fueled by the stories in magazines and newspapers. Usually, I could get some pretty accurate information, not from executives, but from a foreman in Custodial whose was a studio secretary. A persistent rumor which was actually *more* than a rumor was that Disney would be sold off in parts, like a side of beef. Disneyland would be sold to the highest bidder.

People wondered if the new owners would be able to cancel union agreements and lower pay rates and benefits. Key executives could realistically be worried about their futures, and the insecurity spread throughout the park, to all permanent people.

After what seemed an eternity of confusion, Disneyland could finally announce it was "under new management", and the nightmare became the beginning of a new era for the Magic Kingdom.

"If My Boss Calls"

It was the worst of times, but fortunately there were those who helped with what is called "gallows humor". As an example, I think of Bob Risteen, our finance director, who should have been "in the know".

His instructions to his secretary were: "If my boss calls, be sure to get his name so I can call him back."

PART EIGHT

The New Era
1987–

FIFTY-FIVE

Everything Turned Up Roses

In a way, my Disneyland career had started in Fort Worth, Texas, where I'd met Wood. And now the eyes of Texas were on Disneyland.

The company announced that the billionaire Bass Brothers of Texas had purchased controlling interest in Walt Disney Productions.

Walt's nephew, Roy Disney, Jr., was a member of the new Board of Directors, and it was announced that the company would be held together under the direction of two competent executives: Michael Eisner and Frank Wells.

The new management couldn't have picked a better time to take over, particularly at Disneyland. Those terrible strikes were behind us, and some of our costs were contained. The crowds who stayed away in 1984 because of the Summer Olympics now came to Disneyland in droves. And then...1985.

Everything in 1985 turned up roses for the new management:

- It was our 30th anniversary year, and the publicity hoopla was bigger than ever.
- We exceed the 12 million mark for yearly attendance for the first time in history.
- Under our new Touchstone label, the hit movie *Splash* had made money for the old management. Now, for the new guys, a series of box-office winner began, with *Down and Out in Beverly Hills*.
- We were back on TV with a hit Disney sitcom, the award-winning *Golden Girls*.
- The stockholders were happy: Disney stock went up, split, and went up again.
- Videopolis was added to Fantasyland for stage shows to attract teens.
- New live shows were created to bring back local visitors.

- Profits at Disneyland, Walt Disney World, and Tokyo Disneyland were better than ever.

- Many of our Disneyland people were happy with the new era, although it was not 100%, not by a damn sight...

In addition to being a president of Walt Disney World and Disneyland, Dick was a member of the Disney Board of Directors. Thus, he had been part of the high-level wheeling and dealing. Now he called a meeting at 8 in the morning in the Lincoln Theatre. Nobody stayed away.

The new top executives were not present at this session. Dick expressed confidence in the new management and explained how they had been long-time admirers of Walt Disney. He even came up with an apt description for this dynamic team: "They walk fast."

An additional series of meetings was scheduled for all Disneylanders at the Space Stage in Tomorrowland. Dick handled the introductions and gave an excellent introduction of these two "fast walkers" who would now control our destiny:

- Michael Eisner, the new chairman of the board, had come to Disney after being president of Paramount Pictures during their most successful years.

- Frank Wells had been president of Warner Brothers before he took a year off to climb six of the seven highest mountains in the world.

Both Michael and Frank reassured us that they had full confidence in our theme park management under Dick Nunis and Ron Dominguez.

At the end of the session, the new executives lined up to shake hands with everyone present, and we all went back to work.

It was end of a long mid-life crisis. Now...what would the future bring?

A much-used phrase at this time of change was "culture shock". For some of us old-timers, it was closer to "culture rupture".

Walt and Roy were two Midwest boys who believed in the family audience. They built Disneyland to reflect their values. Now the control of the company had passed to a team of brilliant, highly educated, sophisticated men backed by money-smart investors.

I was to be asked more frequently if this or that would happen "if Walt were alive", and heard much more talk about the "good old days", which, as you know, were not always so damned good.

Despite the doubters, there was a new vibrancy throughout the Disney Company. Names were changed. "Walt Disney Productions" became "The Walt Disney Company". I still have trouble trouble saying "Walt Disney Imagineering" instead of "WED" for our design firm.

Some couldn't adapt to change, and others ended up with better jobs. Some took "early retirement", reducing my circle of friends.

I tried to focus on the many positive changes. And fortunately, Dick made it possible for me to realize a dream I'd been cultivating for about 30 years.

FIFTY-SIX

A Trip to Walt's Roots

I was adjusting to the new management when Dick asked me to come to Florida to help on the training program for EPCOT Center.

With all the changes, my mind had been going back to our Disney roots. Rather than flying to Florida, I asked Dick if my wife and I could get there by way of Walt's boyhood home in Marceline, Missouri. He understood my interest and approved it.

Why was I interested in Marceline? I'll explain.

Back in 1955, I was absorbing everything I could about Walt. Marceline, I learned, was his boyhood home. And, in various interviews, he remembered that town with his fondest memories.

In my World's Fair handbook, I mentioned that it was the home where he had first drawn a horse for one dollar. Months later, Dolores Wheeler, Roy Disney's secretary, sent me a note. She liked the handbook, but admonished me that "Marceline is in Missouri, not Ohio. And he was paid only 25 cents for drawing the horse. In those days, you could *buy* a horse for a dollar."

On the night after Walt's death, at our wake in the Disneyland Hotel, Jack Olsen said, "Disneyland is the road map of Walt Disney's life." From everything I'd read about the man, I could see parts of his life reproduced at Disneyland. His boyhood home in Marceline was present in many things: the berm, the railroad, the landscaping, the rivers, the horse-drawn vehicles, the band. They were Walt's memories.

Although he'd also lived in Chicago and Kansas City, it was to Marceline that he and Roy would go for a special celebration. Of course, his WED research team had studied other Midwestern towns, but Walt's imprint had to be of his days in Marceline.

My wife and I made reservations on Amtrak to Kansas City, Missouri. We chugged and clickety-clacked our way to a station which must have been there during Walt's Kansas City days.

At that time, Hallmark Cards had its headquarters in Kansas City. Before I left California I checked with their local representative, and he called his boss to arrange for our visit. In the hotel room when we arrived was a box of goodies and a book about Kansas City, including tales of Walt's days when he was in business there.

I called this Hallmark executive to find out the best way to get to Marceline. He was pleasant, helpful, invited us to tour Hallmark. Certainly he had been to Marceline many times. But my request surprised him, and his response was, "Marceline? Where the hell is Marceline?" He'd never heard of the town.

We checked our maps, found the right highway, and headed east. On the way, we passed the boyhood hoods of General George Pershing and J.C. Penney. Finally, and we almost missed it, was a small sign proclaiming, "Marceline, Boyhood Home of Walt Disney".

I drove down the main street of Marceline/Disneyland. I was not disappointed.

We had breakfast in the only little café which was open. I remember it well: hotcakes, two eggs, bacon, orange juice, coffee, milk, more coffee—all for $1.10.

Walt Disney Park was a disappointment. The track for our old Viewliner was there, but if Walt had seen the place, somebody would have been fired... immediately!

We asked questions and found the house where Walt had lived with his four brothers and a sister. The trees and landscaping might have been as they were back in 1910 But the house looked modern. It was freshly painted, and had been upgraded by its previous owners. At the front door was one of those speaker things, as you might find at the entrance to a gated apartment complex.

We pressed the bell, but there was no answer.

And that was it: short on time, and with nothing else to do, I walked away from Walt's old home, after all the time it took me to get there, and got back on the road to Florida, where Dick and I finalized our discussion of the new training program, and I turned right around and flew back to Disneyland.

But now, whenever I walk down Main Street, U.S.A., I think of Main Street, Marceline, and that $1.10 breakfast.

FIFTY-SEVEN

The Spirit of Disneyland

Over the years, the University of Disneyland continued to grow. And although I report directly to Dick, my basic functions have most often been controlled by the manager of the university. This position has been a career springboard for every manager with whom I've worked.

In every case, these managers were bright, dedicated, and possessed of another quality which was most important to me: they didn't treat me as a doddering old-timer, but rather, we would share ideas and they would include me in planning programs. Bill Ross was the thoughtful manager during the park's mid-life crisis and the strikes. Over a pancake breakfast, we reviewed some of our past university programs:

- "You'll Create Happiness" had been the theme for pre-opening and the early years.
- "You and the Disneyland Show" had established us as the professionals in outdoor entertainment.
- "The Traditions of Walt Disney at Disneyland" held us together after Walt's death.

Each of these programs had been directed at specific objectives, such as maintaining a dedicated, competent, and courteous group of Disneyland cast members. And now we were challenged to come up with a plan which would counteract some real problems, such as:

There were those who were apprehensive about the new top management, and had accepted a "just a job" defense until they could reach retirement.

The strikes had increased the breach between management, the unions, and other hourly personnel. And there was a breakdown between friends, a resentment by those who had walked the picket lines to the bitter end, and those who had returned to work before a final settlement.

With these morale problems, it was hard to sell happiness and pixie dust. But selling those things was our entire reason for being—our purpose and our product.

Having just returned from Marceline, I had a new transfusion of Disney blood. I was convinced that management and owners could come and go, but that Walt's dream would last forever. The Vatican had survived under many popes. The (actual) White House had survived many presidents. And the spirit and traditions of Disneyland were surviving in Florida and in Tokyo.

On about the third cup of coffee, we came up with a theme of "The Spirit of Disneyland". It was intangible, but reflected a certain dedication which many of us felt. We presented the idea to Dick, who was well aware of our morale problems, and he liked it. In fact, he became very involved and it was "Charge!".."Damn the Budget!"..."Full Speed Ahead!"

We scheduled a meeting at the Lincoln Theatre where Dick and Ron Dominguez would present "The Spirit of Disneyland". The previous meeting we'd had at this location was the one where Dick had told us about the new top management. A lot had ridden on that meeting, and a lot was riding on this one, too. We wanted people to glance back at our unique history and look forward to what would be an exciting future.

Even though some of the people who worked on the new program hadn't been alive when Disneyland opened, they'd somehow absorbed Walt's ideals and values, and the program they created was proof that the "spirit" of Disneyland was alive and well.

The future was in good hands...and hearts and minds, too. I was touched.

Dorothy Eno advised me that Dick wanted to see me in this office at 8 in the morning...before the park opened. I thought he wanted to discuss business. Instead, when I came into the office he stood and said, "Let's take a walk."

We walked out toward the Inn Between, our cast cafeteria, and then we headed down Main Street. And there, gathered in front of the Tobacco Shop, was the Disneyland Band and a group of my friends and colleagues. Craig Smith was there with Ron Dominguez. And then Dick said some nice words and unveiled a window with the inscription:

> VAN ARSDALE FRANCE
> FOUNDER AND
> PROFESSOR EMERITUS
> DISNEY UNIVERSITIES

I probably said the wrong thing, although I forget what. The band played—fortunately *not* "The Old Grey Mare—and then we moved to Dick's office where I received a bottle of scotch labeled "Spirit of Disneyland".

Craig Smith told me later that at first they were going to put the window above the Candy Shop, but since I'm one of the few remaining smokers at Disneyland, they thought that putting it above the Tobacco Shop was more appropriate.

It was a memorable morning.. I think I went home and had a good cry.

FIFTY-EIGHT

The Disneyland Alumni Club

The saying that "you can take the boy out of the country, but you can't take the country out of the boy" has an application at Disneyland.

We have a club for people who have retired – the "Golden Ears Club". It's an active group which gets together every month. Last time I checked, there were nearly 200,000 people who had worked at Disneyland and then left, for whatever reason.

My status was unique. First, I'd quit at one time, and knew what it was like to be outside the berm, but still interested in Disneyland. And second, I was half-retired and half-working. Once again, Wally Boag, the famous Top Banana of the Golden Horseshoe Revue, came up with an idea.

Wally had taken early retirement and invited me to see the fancy office where he was working and have lunch. We talked about Disneyland and the "old days" and the "new days" and decided to get some of our friends together and, as an afterthought, form a club.

I worked up a plan and presented it to Dick, who liked the idea. Some of the working executives didn't really understand it, since they had never been "out" looking in. But, with a small group and a lot of help from Dick and Bob Baldwin, Director of the Magic Kingdom Club, we sailed ahead.

We developed a magazine, and our first major event was a reunion party for the 30th Disneyland anniversary. It was a grand mixture of early pioneers (even C.V. Wood showed up) and younger people who might have only worked with us for one summer.

FIFTY-NINE

And the Trees Grow More Beautiful Every Year

Disneyland is something that will never be finished. It's alive. It will be a living, breathing thing that will need change. A picture is a thing, once you wrap it up and turn it over to Technicolor, you're through. I wanted something alive, something that could grow. Not only can I add things, but even the trees will grow and become more beautiful each year.

— Walt Disney

I'm writing this from my office/trailer in Disneyland's Circle D Ranch. This is where our "cast" of horses is housed, trained, and pampered.

To get here, I usually walk from the Administration Building down Main Street, then across the moat through Fantasyland, and through a "For Cast Members Only" gate to backstage.

Frequently, I'll pause to watch the swans in the moat, and as I pass through the entrance to Sleeping Beauty Castle, I always take the time to listen to "When You Wish Upon a Star", which has been playing since we opened.

My favorite time is early in the morning before the park opens, when the guests – God bless 'em – have not yet arrived to distract me. I can take the time to look around and enjoy the many creative architectural wonders which can be found in this wondrous place.

Just a few days ago, I looked *up* in Fantasyland – at the clocks, weather vanes, and other treasures I'd never taken the time to see before.

And the tress! Walt was prophetic when he said that these would become more beautiful every year. My favorites are what I think of as my "pioneer" trees. These are the ones we saved from death by freeway construction back in 1955. Like me, they weren't young when they were relocated here, and each one has a distinct personality. They may be as old as I am. I feel like saluting them with, "Hi, Old-Timer!"

The early morning is also a great time to chat with my friends who are working on final park clean-up or preparing to open our shops for the rush of guests who will soon arrive.

Often, while I've been struggling to wrap up this story, I reflect on what a wonderful inheritance Walt left me, as well as a few hundred million others, to enjoy. He said Disneyland was a "work of love", and I believe that. I'm convinced that he often thought of his boyhood in Marceline, Missouri, when he was designing and operating his dream. He certainly believed in our goal of creating happiness for others, and I have living proof of that.

At this time of year, there is a special beauty at Disneyland. All of our lights and decorations are up for Christmas, just as Walt wanted it.

My grandson, Ryan, and my granddaughter, Stacey, have been talking about a trip to Disneyland for eight months. I'll get a chance to see my happy place through *their* eyes as well as through my own.

Yes. The concept of happiness for others is still alive and well, and like the trees will survive for many more decades.

I've been lucky to be a part of it.

THE END

Van France has "Robin Hood" exactly where he wants him, at sword-point on a battlement of Sleeping Beauty Castle, in Disneyland.

Van teaching a fresh ensemble of cast members about Disney traditions.

Van France, during the heyday of his Disney career, with the "Beautiful Disney Tradition", that he helped to create, behind him.

DISNEYLAND
A Division of Walt Disney Productions

INTER-OFFICE COMMUNICATION
D-102

TO ___DICK NUNIS_____ DATE____NOVEMBER 8, 1982_____

FROM___VAN FRANCE_____ SUBJECT__FLORIDA TRIP/MARCELINE____

DICK...

Here's a diary of our trip from Disneyland to Walt Disney World.
You should read the part on Marceline. I have recommendations:

1. There is nothing worse than an abandoned Midget Autopia. And,
   I don't know who approved the park sign. We or they should
   spend the money to tear out the remains and leave in grass.

2. Or, we might subsidise the local Junior Chamber of Commerce in
   order to have the place properly maintained, and the "Boyhood
   Home" sign improved.

VAN

Fresh from his junket to Florida and Walt Disney's childhood home-
town of Marceline, Missouri, Van has some recommendations for
his boss, Dick Nunis, in this Disneyland inter-office memo.

A dapper Van in front of Sleeping Beauty Castle.

Van between fellow Disney Legends: animator and later Imagineer Bill Justice on the left, and landscaper Morgan "Bill" Evans on the right.

A group shot of Club 55 members taken during Disneyland's 35th anniversary celebration. (Club 55 is for cast members who were employed at Disneyland in 1955.) Van is in the front row, sixth from the left. The rest:

Third Row
Dick Nunis, Bob Penfield, Dominic Conte, Homer Holland, Jim Quigley, Scotty Cribbes, Arnold Lindberg, Jack Taylor, Ray VanDeWarker, Jack Lindquist, Chuck Boyajian, Cal McMurtry, Ron Dominguez

Second Row
Tom Roppa, Milo Rainey, Tom Nabbe, Harold Christopher, Gunter Otto, Al Alvarez, Dale Drummond, John Catone, George Short, Hank Dains, Bill "Sully" Sullivan, Bud Washo.

First Row
Broney Ceisluk, Ron Heminger, Frank Martinez, Cora Lee Sargeant, Meg Lyles, Van France, Jim Cashen, Milt Albright, Ed Winger, Ray Swartz.

Van receives his Club 55 ring from John Catone, who got his start at Disneyland mingling with Tomorrowland guests while wearing a space suit. He rose through the ranks to become Disneyland's Manager of Communication Services.

Van with former Dick Nunis. Van hired Dick as his "gofer" back in 1955. Dick went on to become Van's boss, and eventually the chairman of Walt Disney Attractions.

Van and Dick Nunis hold up a replica of Van's window on Main Street. It reads: "Van Arsdale France. Founder and Professor Emeritus, Disney Universities.".

Van's actual window on Main Street, in Disneyland, above the 20th Century Music Shop. It was originally above the long-gone Disneyland Tobacco Shop, a more appropriate location given Van's ever-present cigarette.

A later shot of Van with Dick Nunis. The inscription reads: "Van, Thank you for the memories. You have been my mentor, but most of all my friend. Dick Nunis."

Becoming a Disney Legend can be a messy affair. Van holds up his muddy hands while kneeling between fellow Legends Jack Lindquist (left) and Bill Cottrell. Lindquist retired from the company as the president of Disneyland; Cottrell as the president of Retlaw Enterprises (Walt's family corporation) after a long stint as the first president of Walt Disney Imagineering.

Van stands next to the imprint of his hands, framed there after his Disney Legend induction ceremony.

Acknowledgments

My story is the story of thousands of pioneers, characters, friends, colleagues, and cronies who have touched me, from a hug to a "hello", and I say THANK YOU to:

Chuck and Nonna Abbott; Milt, Maggie, and June Albright; Bob, Rolley and "Bubba" Allen; Al Alvarez; Earl Anderson; Leo Ara; Lee Acuff; Arthur Adler; Jose Arias; Elaine Anderson; Betty Appleton; Ralph Adams; Earl Archer; Ken Anderson; Jerry Arzeroni; Jim Barngrover; Dave Bartchard; Joyce Belanger; Wally, Ellen and Laurence Boag; Chuck Boyajian; Roy Brehm; Imogene Brinkmeyer; Charley Brock; Rima and Bob Bruce; Stan Bailey; Charlotte Ballard; Tony Baxter; Harold Bastrup; Ruth Bartling; Phil Bauer; Alexis Beauvais; Jim Benedick; Bill Berry; Virginia Bixler; Cap Blackbum; Audrey Blasdell; Hank Block; Dorothy Bradley; Jack Breslin; Jack Brown; Paul Brewer; Betty Taylor; Fulton Burley; Mark Brush; John Buckie; Chuck Bums; Woodrow Butterfield; Bob Baldwin; Renie Bardeau; Chuck Boyer; Jay Brilliantes; Gail Brown; Roger Broggie; Richard Battaglia; Walt Bricker; Roger Banner; Edsel Barrett; Jim Cashen; John Catone; Art Chapman; Chris ·christopher; Broney Ciesluk; Dominic Conte; Lucy Cottom; Scotty Cribbs; Pete Crimmings; Doc Campbell; Della Carr; Bonnie Cartwright; Mel Cecil; Blair Clark; Donna Clark; John Cohen; Susan Cora; Chuck Corson; Ted Crowell; Charles Courier; Valerie Watson Curry; ·Jim Gashin; Dottie Chatfield; Gina Climer; Garry Conk; Jim Cora; John Cora; Colin Campbell; Larry Celmons; Claude Coates; Virl Casey; Edgar Carnegie; Paul Castle; Clint Crittendon; Pete Clark; Bud and Betty Coulson; Ruth Cowan; Vern Croft; Bing Crosby (our Bing); Ted Crowell; John Collins; Dorothy Cartwright; Hank Dains; Dario D'amore; Joe Delphin; Boyd Diaz; Ron and Betty Dominguez; James Dacey; Bob Daniel; John Davidheiser; Christine Donovan; Andrew Dubill; Jim Dunahm; Jerry Dailey; Bill Davis; Gary Dye; Rainier Dickman; Leon Duty; Marc Davis; Earle Dandie; Lee David; Bob Davis; Don Defore; Wes Demons; Roy Doyle; Hubert Drummond; Fred and Dana Duffy; Dorothy and Dick Eno; Bill Evans; Tom Eastman; Lella Easton; John Edwards; Fred Elder; Ed Ettinger; Don Edgren; Jim Eason; Dawn Esposito; Joe Fowler; W.C. Fields; Frank Forsythe; Jean France; Gary Fravel; Irene Fleetwood; Al Flores; Orlando Ferrante; Hugo Fardin; Carl

Ereeberg; Jim Garber; Art Gardner; John Gerlach; Terry Gilres; John Gray; Dick Galentine; Oren Gallegly; John Gerlock; Cecil Gibson; Stan Gomez; Al Grills; Deidre Glaser; Bob Gault; Anita Gray; Ken Grinstead; Louie Gordon; Teri Goss; John Hernandez; Bill Hoelscher; Homer Holland; Vivian Gerlach Hadley; Sara Hanlon; Gary Hare; Jim Harmon; Ann Harber; Paula Hasler; Patty Hastreiter; Gerald Hefferly; Reed Heilson; Ronalq Heminger; Martha Henderson; Jim Hilinski; Lee Hively; Helen Holliday; Barbara How; Lawrence Hutchinson; Kathy Helgeson; Lisa Hiat; John Hench; Frank Hideo; Chuck Hannaford; Derris Hensley; Thin Hahne; Joel Halberstadt, Bob Hanna, Vera Hanson; Frank Heidemann; Glenn Hicks; Lee Hight; Clint Hill; Clarice Higgins; Don Hufstader; Sharon Hufstader; Vern Holland; Bill Hansen; Harry Hamhauser; Connie Hallaheen; Mary Jane Homs; Margaret Homer; Rich Irvine; Ike Isaacson; Merrill Jacobs; Freda and Jack Jacobson; Charlie and Vicki Jiminez; Bea Jones; Dick Johnson; Len Jones; Tom Jacobson; Judy Justus; Fran Kay; Steve Kasper; Jack Kehoe; Foreset Kimler; Edie Klar; Jan Knowlton; Dave Koch; George Kohlenberger; Gary Kirk; Ken Kohler; Ron Kollen; Bob Kumamoto; Tom Keene; Ward Kimball; Dick Korn; Herman Kneip; Greg King; Arnold Lindberg; Jack and Belle Lindquist; Mig Lyles; Bob Laubacher; Shirley Lawler; Armand Levi; David Lancashire; Lee Loman; Stan La Fortune; George Le Febre; Jo Leeper; Eugene "Doc" Lemmon; Mike· Larson; Dottie Livingston; Prank Martines; Cal McMurtry; Bob Milek; Lulu Miller; George Mills, Sr.; George Mills, Jr.; Mabel McKibbin; Frank McNeil; Dave Melanson; Joanne Miller; Tom Mitchell; Jim Moran; Becky Morris; Linda Morse; Al Mutke; Tom Naabe; Andrea Manes; Kathy Mangum; Bob Mathieson; Gail Matsunaga; Ginger Mccollum; Bob McHenry; Mike McKeever; Beverly and Darrel Metzger; Mary Anne Mang; Joyce McMahon; Bob McTyre; Tom Meslovich; Mat Mew; Sharon Miller; Sebastian Moreno; Sam McKim; Ben Meister; John Miller; Ron Miller; Tom Mitchell; William Moyer; Bill Martin; Eddie Meck; Joe Meck; Ed Mackie; Millie Malley; Francis Marinkovich; Dick May; Jim McCurry; George Meggs; Laura Morgan; Becky Morris; Jane McGee; Dean Narath; Dick, June, Rich, Lesa and Mary Nunis; Tom Nabbe; Al Neimeyer; Larry Nunes; Bud Nagel; Evelyn Nelson; Charlie Nichols; Mary Neynaber; Arthur Narath; Fred Newcomb; Jack and Marty Olsen; Gunter Otto; Mike O'Brien; Tim O'Day; Michey Orossco; Chuck Ousley; Bob Penfield; Dean Penlick; Frank Pfannenstein; Gil Pimentel; Dolly and Owen Pope; Van Pagdalaskas; Ethel Penfield; Bob Phelps; Skip Palmer; Jim Pasilla; Chris and Lois Portillo; Nick Paccione; Terry Plantamura; Jim Quigley; "Mondo" Vermondo Libro Quaglia; Paul Quade; Gary Quale; Milo Rainey; Tom and Rose Roppa; Jaynette Rasmussen; Lee Reineke; Sal Restivo; Frank Reynolds; Charlie Ridgway; Chris Ridgway; Carl Ritter; Chuck Romero; Dona Rochelle; Richard Ramsey; Cicely Rigdon; Bill Ross; Bob Roth; Herb

Ryman; Jack Reilly; Trinidad Ruiz; Bob and Vinnie Reilly; Cora Lee Sargent; Marion Schwacha; Anne Salisbwy; Cori Sandoval; Ricci Schollar; Jeff and Yem Sherman; Chuck Sheilds; Susan Sietez; John Sipes; Lucy Smeltzer; Bob Smith; Rich Sowder; John Stewart; Ken St. Hill; Vicki Stowe; Connie Swanson; Ron Swartz; Day Sechler; Bruce Siriani; Ken Slezak; Stan Sowa; Tom Stabille; Richard Stovall; Gil Scamecchia; Craig Smith; Marty Sklar; Ray Schwartz; George Short; John Stevenson; Bill Sullivan; Maynard Swenson; Tommy Scheid; Dianna Stark; Larry Smith; Andy Saravyn; Larry Snow; Virginia Swan; Reva Stewart; Betty Schroeder; Jan Stenson; Bob Tafoya; Tom Tancredi; Camille Tedesco; Donn Tatum; Burt Taylor; Mary Theil; Owen Tiedy; Frank Turner; Charlotte Turpin; Jack Taylorp Fred Tatum; Ted Tracy; Jim Umstead; Arlyce Underwood; Dave Vermeulen; Esther Vaughn; Tony Virginia; Ray Van de Warker; Mary Van Thyme; Earl Vilmer; Terry Votaw; Jck Wagner; Bert Walker; Tommy Walker; Bill Weigle; Dick Wells; Jerry White; Eve Wilhelm; Roy Williams; Sharon Woodruff; Truman Woodworth; Wilbur Wright; Laraine Wright; John Waite; Bob Warren; Estelle Webb; Susan Webb; Jon Webb; Mary Wormhoudt; Mary Jo Wilson; Bettie Woody; Garry Wood; Bud Washo; George Williams; Ed Winger; Woody Woodsworth; Earl Wuestneck; Clifford Walker; Vesey Walker; Chuck Whelan; Walt Walno; Eddie Wisniewiski; Bill Weaver.

Also to my darling Stel Webb: thank you for 35 wonderful years together. You have been my best friend and the most patient "free" editor that I could ask for and I will always love you.

And, since I forgot to name my daughter, Cheryl France, who worked as a ticket hostess, I may have missed some others who I thank, once again, for the memories.

Oh, and thanks for the dream, Walt.

More Books from Theme Park Press

Theme Park Press publishes dozens of books each year for Disney fans and for general and academic audiences. Here are just a few of our titles. For the complete catalog, including book descriptions and excerpts, please visit:

ThemeParkPress.com

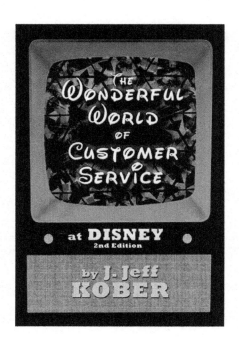

50 YEARS IN THE MOUSE HOUSE

The Lost Memoir of One of Disney's Nine Old Men

ERIC LARSON

Edited by Didier Ghez and Joe Campana

DISNEY'S GRAND TOUR

WALT AND ROY'S EUROPEAN VACATION
SUMMER 1935

DIDIER GHEZ

From Disneyland's
Tom Sawyer
to Disney Legend

The Adventures of Tom Nabbe

TOM NABBE

From
Jungle Cruise Skipper
to Disney Legend

40 Years of Magical Memories at Disney

William "Sully" Sullivan

Walt Disney
AND THE PROMISE OF
Progress City

SAM GENNAWEY
Foreword by Werner Weiss

INSIDE THE DISNEY
MARKETING
MACHINE

In the Era of
Michael Eisner & Frank Wells

Lorraine Santoli
Foreword by Sam Tuchman, Ph.D.

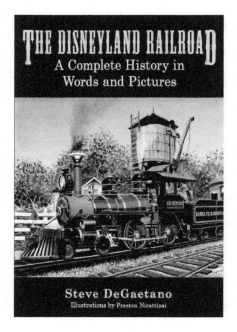

THE DISNEYLAND RAILROAD
A Complete History in
Words and Pictures

Steve DeGaetano
Illustrations by Preston Nirattisai

Great Big
Beautiful
Tomorrow

Walt Disney
and Technology

Christian Moran
with Rolly Crump,
Bob Gurr, Jim Korkis,
Sam Gennawey and Dr.
Maureen Furniss, Ph.D.

It's A
CRAZY BUSINESS

The
GOOFY
Life of a
Disney
Legend

Pinto Colvig

Edited and Introduced by Todd James Pierce

EVERYTHING
I KNOW
I LEARNED FROM
DISNEY ANIMATED
FEATURE FILMS

Advice for Living Happily Ever After

JIM KORKIS

Author of
The Vault of Walt

A Disney Historian FUN FACT Book

MOUSE IN
TRANSITION

An Insider's Look at
Disney Feature Animation

STEVE HULETT

Foreword by John Musker
Disney Feature Films Animation Director

Disneyland
SECRETS

GAVIN DOYLE

Made in the USA
Monee, IL
08 January 2020

20053374R10125